# How to Catch a Phish

## A Practical Guide to Detecting Phishing Emails

Nicholas Oles

Apress®

***How to Catch a Phish: A Practical Guide to Detecting Phishing Emails***

Nicholas Oles
Severn, MD, USA

ISBN-13 (pbk): 978-1-4842-9360-7 ISBN-13 (electronic): 978-1-4842-9361-4
https://doi.org/10.1007/978-1-4842-9361-4



Managing Director, Apress Media LLC: Welmoed Spahr
Acquisitions Editor: Susan McDermott
Development Editor: Laura Berendson
Coordinating Editor: Jessica Vakili
Copy Editor: Kim Burton

Distributed to the book trade worldwide by Springer Science+Business Media New York, 233 Spring Street, 6th Floor, New York, NY 10013. Phone 1-800-SPRINGER, fax (201) 348-4505, e-mail orders-ny@springer-sbm.com, or visit www.springeronline.com. Apress Media, LLC is a California LLC and the sole member (owner) is Springer Science + Business Media Finance Inc (SSBM Finance Inc). SSBM Finance Inc is a **Delaware** corporation.

For information on translations, please e-mail booktranslations@springernature.com; for reprint, paperback, or audio rights, please e-mail bookpermissions@springernature.com.

Apress titles may be purchased in bulk for academic, corporate, or promotional use. eBook versions and licenses are also available for most titles. For more information, reference our Print and eBook Bulk Sales web page at http://www.apress.com/bulk-sales.

Any source code or other supplementary material referenced by the author in this book is available to readers on the Github repository: https://github.com/Apress/How-to-Catch-a-Phish. For more detailed information, please visit http://www.apress.com/source-code.

Printed on acid-free paper

# Table of Contents

# About the Author

**Nick Oles** is a cybersecurity expert with over 15 years of operational experience in military, industry, and academic environments. He has worked on incident response and threat hunting teams and consulted with Fortune 150 organizations, small businesses, and US Department of Defense entities. Nick has served his country for over a decade in the cyber and special operations communities, earning multiple military accolades, completing worldwide deployments, and serving in joint special operations environments. He has advised award-winning academic centers on cyber-program development and management, as well as created and taught academic and certification courses on a variety of cybersecurity topics. Nick has detected, analyzed, and responded to thousands of security incidents over his career. He continues to actively contribute to the cybersecurity community and teach students at all skill levels while still serving his country.

# About the Technical Reviewer

**Ron Scott** is a former coder, professor, rock climber, and mountain biker, and is currently working for a non-profit in Cleveland, Ohio, that supports people as they strive to become economically self-sufficient.

# Acknowledgements

I would have never completed this book, or much of anything frankly, without the support of my beautiful wife, children, and parents. I've stood on the shoulders of giants, and I thank all my mentors, friends, and weekend warrior Fernandez boys for the continuous stream of poorly crafted insults, coaching, and occasional encouragement along the way. I wasn't always the smartest person in the room, but I was always the best looking.

CHAPTER 1

# How Email Works

Everyone wants to save the world one click at a time, but before traveling down the road of the interwebs and dodging dangerous international hackers, to protect yourself, you need to understand how electronic messages (also known as *email*) work. Email is one of the top forms of communication in the twenty-first century, and its use continues to grow rapidly. With this rapid growth has been a continuous increase in the use of email to trick users and deliver malicious software. Understanding the basic components of an email message and its path from the sender to the recipient can pay exorbitant dividends to you as the network defender, end user, or helpful friend lending a hand. Most likely, every reader of this book has sent and received an email message at some point in your technical or personal career. Although the use and platform vary for each user, the process of sending a message using a mail application remains constant. Let's start where it all begins: the application or program used for email messages.

## Understanding Email Architecture

Email messages require applications (also known as programs) that enable the ability to create, send, and receive messages. These applications come in two main forms: a desktop and a web application. A desktop application is installed, run, and resourced by the local computer to provide email functionality. The web application is running on a web


N. Oles, *How to Catch a Phish*, https://doi.org/10.1007/978-1-4842-9361-4_1

server. All functionality is available through the website, and resources for using email are provided by the web server. Both of these applications are also referred to as mail clients.

The most common mail clients are available in both web and desktop application forms. These include mail providers such as Gmail, Outlook, Yahoo!, and for some of our more seasoned Internet users, AOL(if you don't know, look this one up). Both web and desktop applications typically contain similar functionality and features to the end user. It is usually the "shooter's preference," meaning individuals choose their preferred mail provider and client. Unfortunately, clients do not work autonomously and need connected infrastructure and devices to send and receive electronic messages. All mail, regardless of application or provider, must be routed through a series of servers, starting with the sender and ending with the recipient.

A picture is worth a thousand words, and explaining the concept of email traffic is no exception. The flowchart in Figure 1-1 (from How It Works) shows how email messages traverse networking devices from your mail application as the sender to the recipient's mailbox as the receiver. The following explains each step in more detail.

## Step 1

The message is composed in the mail application. This is where you—the sender—open the email and input an email message. This includes the recipient's email address, the subject, a brief description of the email message, and the body—the content of the message. The mail client should preconfigure the sender's address. Once you click the Send button, the message disappears and begins a mystical journey.

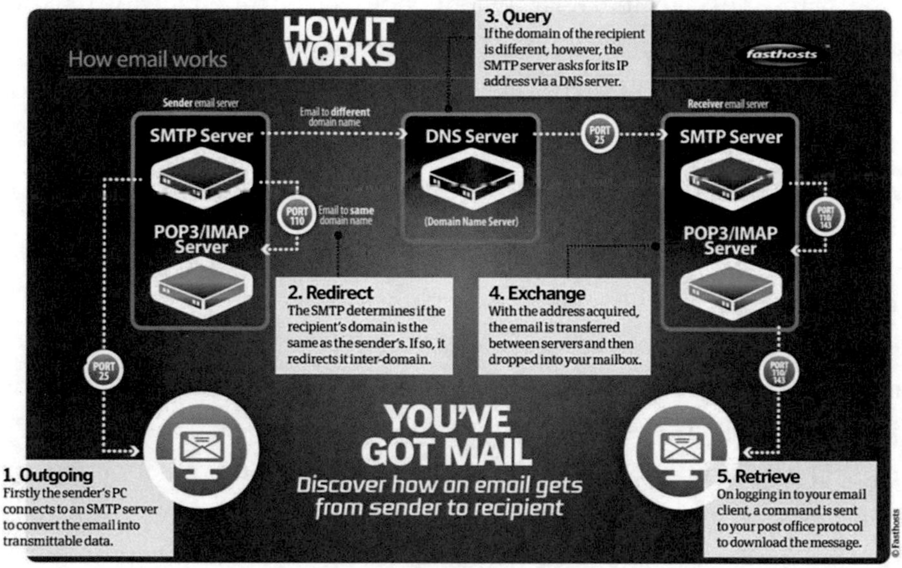


***Figure 1-1.*** *From* *www.howitworksdaily.com/how-does-email-work/*

# Step 2

The sender's email server is always the first stop for your email message. This can be a Windows or Linux server, and communication from your device to the sending email server is done over port 25 using the protocol Simple Mail Transport Protocol, or SMTP. Ports are only discussed briefly in this section, the overall concept is more important than memorizing specific port numbers. The message travels from your desktop through a series of routers and network switches and stops at its first destination—the SMTP server.

Once the SMTP server receives the message, it examines the sender and recipient information. The message is delivered internally if the recipient and the sender are members of the same domain. The domain for email purposes is simply the name after the @ symbol in the email address (@aol.com, @gmail.com, @yahoo.com). For instance, suppose nick@thenetdefender.com sends an email to frank@thenetdefender.com.

Because the message domains (thenetdefender) are the same, the message can be delivered internally. The SMTP server sends the message to a POP3/IMAP server to be delivered to the recipient.

## Step 3

If the sender address and recipient address have different domains, the message needs to be sent out externally through the Internet to be delivered. This would occur if nick@thenetdefender.com sent an email to nick@aol.com. The SMTP server would identify the domains' differences and must resolve the domain @aol.com to an internet protocol (IP) address. Networking equipment on the Internet function on IP addresses instead of domain names. This means the devices resolve and communicate with unique IP addresses; for AOL, this might be 106.10.248.150 or 124.108.115.100. To resolve or look up a particular IP address for a supplied domain name, the SMTP server uses a domain name server, also known as a *DNS server*.

The DNS server operates similarly to a phone book. For those unfamiliar, phone books were physically delivered to every residential home and contained the names and phone numbers of individuals and businesses within the area. This allowed residents to look up an individual or business name and find the associated phone number to call.

A DNS server works similarly but with domain names and IP addresses. For example, a server has no idea where `www.cnn.com` is located or where any email addresses with the domain @cnn.com might be located on the Internet. It must resolve cnn.com to an IP address. The DNS server checks a list of internally stored domains and IP addresses to see if it has a match for cnn.com. If it does, it locates and provides the IP address, which for cnn.com is 151.101.1.67. The DNS server then sends the data packet containing the email message to the appropriate SMTP server identified through the domain to IP address lookup.

## Step 4

The message packet has arrived at the recipient's SMTP server. The path it takes from here is executed in reverse order of the sending mail traffic. After hitting the SMTP server, the data packet travels to the POP3/IMAP server over port 110/143. It then waits on this server for the appropriate mail client to request any new messages and deliver the message.

## Step 5

Contrary to popular belief, a message doesn't simply appear through sorcery and magic in your inbox. Once you open your mail client, the application checks in with the POP3/IMAP server and requests any messages it has for delivery. The POP3/IMAP server checks its mail and delivers any messages stored in the queue for the identified mailbox. It is then delivered to the recipient and downloaded for your viewing pleasure.

Now you know the basic path an email message takes—from the client, through a series of servers and networking devices, to the intended recipient. This happens flawlessly in most cases. But what happens if the recipient's address is mistyped or no longer a valid email address? What if the company closes and or the person has moved on? In this case, the recipient cannot receive the email message; but hopefully, the sender will receive a notification that the email was undeliverable. An undeliverable message is sent to the sender, informing them that the intended recipient's address is invalid. The following are some of the common reasons emails are not delivered.

- Non-existent or mistyped email address
- Recipient's email SMTP server down
- Recipient's mailbox is full and not accepting messages
- Recipient blocked the sender address

Undeliverable messages appear differently depending on the chosen mail client and the reason the mail was not delivered. The issue can often be resolved by confirming the recipient's address and resending the email. Now that you understand the basics of email delivery, let's explore the details of the message beyond the recipient address, subject, and body.

## Email Header and Content

Now that you understand the basic route an email message takes, let's dive deeper into the data associated with the email message. Your computer and networking devices break your intended email message into data packets. The data packets represent small portions of your email separately and are combined to complete your message. As the data packets travel through the various servers and networking devices, they receive and store information on the sender and recipient, the path taken by the email, and any potential errors. This information is stored in the email header, and with a few simple tools, you can help display this information in an easily readable format. First, let's discuss the basics of collecting an email header.

Most of us receive and read emails daily, and are oblivious to the email message header. Accessing the email header takes mere seconds, but the data can sometimes be overwhelming at first glance. The viewing options vary depending on the client and operating system. The next section explains how to view email headers in Outlook, Gmail, and Yahoo! mail platforms. Other platforms follow a similar process, and searching for "viewing email header in XXX mail application", where XXX contains your mail platform, likely results in ample results to aid in your examination.

## Gmail Web Mail

Figure 1-2 is a screenshot of a test email received in the Gmail web application. On the far right are three dots containing more information.

***Figure 1-2.*** *Email in Gmail*

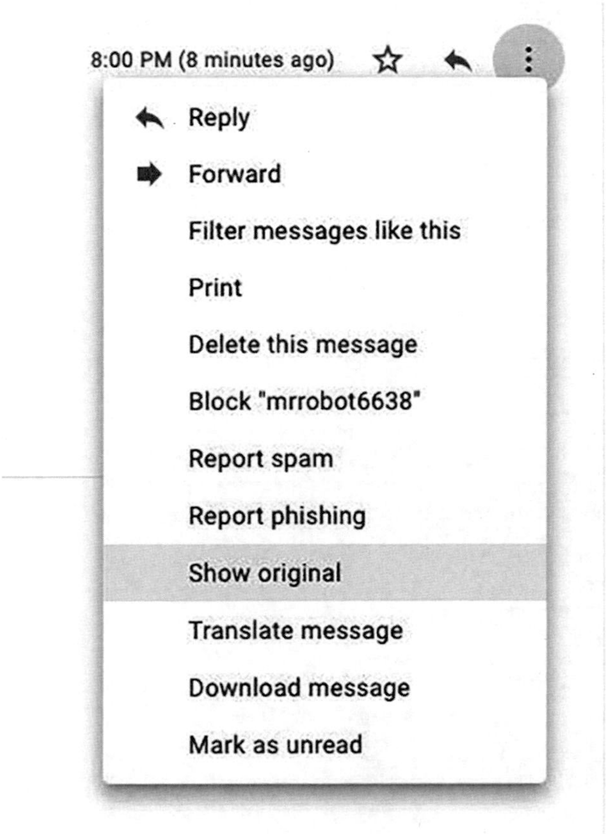


***Figure 1-3.*** *The More options associated with a Gmail message*

Once you have entered the More menu, you can locate and click the Show Original option. This should open a new browser tab and return the results shown in Figure 1-4. You are now accessing the header information for the email you selected. You can follow this process for any message received in the Gmail web application.

***Figure 1-4.*** *Raw email header in Gmail*

# Yahoo! Web Mail Application

Let's start with a similar test email delivered to a Yahoo! mail account (see Figure 1-5).

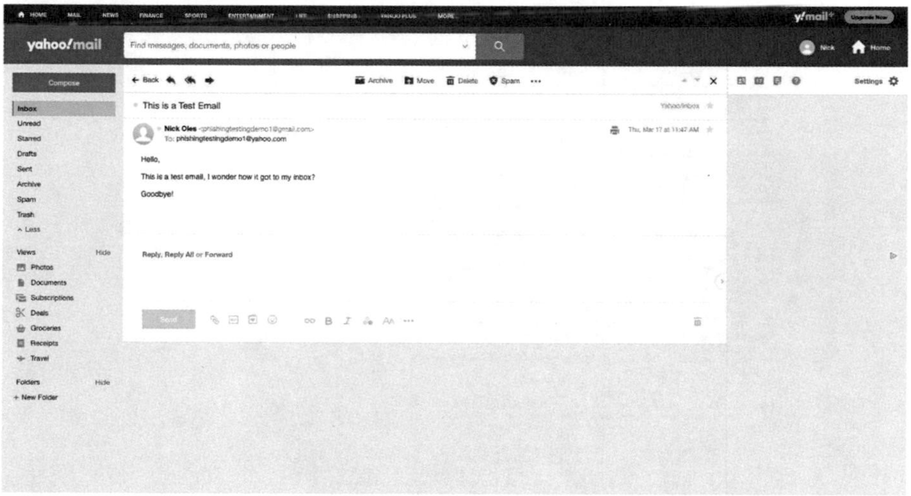


*Figure 1-5. Email screenshot in Yahoo!*

When using Yahoo!, you must locate the More options menu. In Yahoo!, this is located in the center of the page when hovering over the original email. See Figure 1-6 below for a screenshot of a current message, the More options button is in the bottom and center of the page. Once located, you must select the View Raw Message option. This opens the raw message header in a new browser tab.

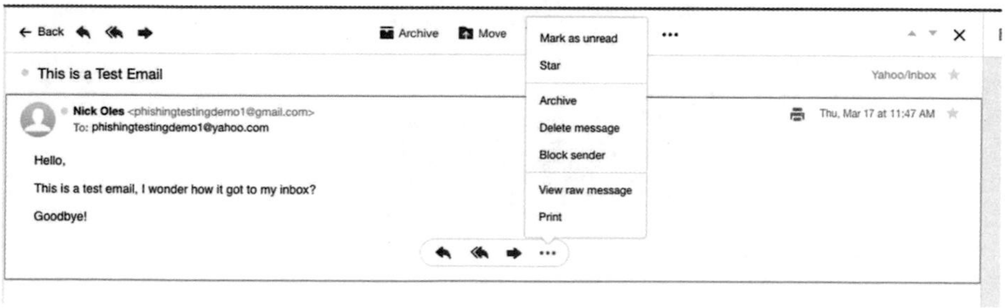


*Figure 1-6. The More menu in Yahoo!*

The raw message header appears similar to the screenshot shown in Figure 1-7. It is important to note that no two messages have the exact raw message header. This information is specific to the data transmitted from this specific email traffic.

```
Received: from 10.253.31.116
 by atlas116.free.mail.gq1.yahoo.com with HTTPS; Thu, 17 Mar 2022 08:47:05 +0000
Return-Path: <phishingtestingdemo1@gmail.com>
X-Originating-Ip: [209.85.219.181]
Received-SPF: pass (domain of gmail.com designates 209.85.219.181 as permitted sender)
Authentication-Results: atlas116.free.mail.gq1.yahoo.com;
 dkim=pass header.i=@gmail.com header.s=20210112;
 spf=pass smtp.mailfrom=gmail.com;
 dmarc=pass(p=NONE,sp=QUARANTINE) header.from=gmail.com;
X-Apparently-To: phishingtestingdemo1@yahoo.com; Thu, 17 Mar 2022 08:47:05 +0000
X-YMailISG: O4gUd9sWLDvjoPVnkFJD.RKJm0NMimi2Zt6ZN4T3_et_E4Mn
 TSGryO8lMMTM94GYiM63gTDNVinkSK3gEKUckwMzWdNmeunNjA5WzIZyymtp
 97YiEENuTf6SqEYqA5pSc.z6qel7wN4VUt2IcM8S7dvXluuFU99N8TGYPQmM
 yEeSReUY8OUbHqR8z.0RCde0NEM7Stvc2gXpMgowOzkgyIxOlWqk8q5p2yKe
 fhaRhFXoNYEVhKpLDOFT0RANVWxtbBnSn6r62CRPwaNURrbQvm4ttlcbfN_T
 ufSEXPHrPURUTWkrt0C9mFdbvTQbBdAiYG8S8cljaNNsmKUJh7kbMpqDeiPC
 nZKeDYlc5GQ7Egyg3p5zpactbBe5mXQ_okzdlaCFU3ARXqs0v6JQ_TBkmvNN
 wEDY4DuPd.Qn0U5uF7coyJ8Bls1ZY50ktzHPS5dlYeEm8UTpg8fcROUdAogS
 n7OtnqzsYtjOCTntITmaB0AioFqB_AdDMI_sk22yn7.r52CANdwc425CjKsN
 TWiRQeXNEgq5sAllx0vgYTm0lIqdhRzJpTto52g9shNaad.NRfoc7ZZjv3hT
 2BfqflvSCrAtXNwj6DwZV2AxPrePyvznxPWxABGI44_eD4ZpivqPc4dlNFoe
 VFpqy2RluKFAlSSuMnBYz4NXEaeN3CcQSnkt.B6Masggdf9Hx_GKKewLFjP7
 9tl9RoXGQsxHdhxeNcKi7piNBlAU3SAunDbr.pQ8EZO8Bzg1h9gB9xSVKoDZ
 1T_rE_LOLwS5zgzbPVVuoropJnzn31Lf3WSDeIdtYmfpk44SlRWse4_t8Of5
 Yed6Nwl4mgE6Yj2Qo.OtD9BvMZpveghcELf7x99FtecX4vaURxQtEIbLVdMc
 t7C_8KA5OQPCLBv58RjSdT6aHNym_fizuUwjJlj7fF9crDAkt85xv0iscXoH
 7TSRjJrvFY._pcPk_RlSVlj3qplr0Zl2DTOrmUWA.JXGIptXKOJVUbM75n6u
 UxhF_BBXKWZXxI6QIhK.hvePZK5A4e7Ftzo9MTPsxJXwnAZe0mWWkPmhVxg_
 J7hMSYV6LCTVHpM303AlmEvayCmImvp4MRFP3zTDIZuB6LVSZEjBm_LNADxF
 ksE_ly0BSC7dELbvfsPmYOdSBT5SxnSw4lpUd3iIKKI-
Received: from 209.85.219.181 (EHLO mail-ybl-f181.google.com)
 by 10.253.31.116 with SMTPs
 (version=TLS1_3 cipher=TLS_AES_128_GCM_SHA256);
 Thu, 17 Mar 2022 08:47:05 +0000
Received: by mail-ybl-f181.google.com with SMTP id 12so8909960ybe.8
        for <phishingtestingdemo1@yahoo.com>; Thu, 17 Mar 2022 01:47:05 -0700 (PDT)
DKIM-Signature: v=1; a=rsa-sha256; c=relaxed/relaxed;
        d=gmail.com; s=20210112;
        h=mime-version:from:date:message-id:subject:to;
        bh=mc57FoW6zrn7Wng6YTURYh5V8x/Z64llQvT+HxMvkRw=;
        b=FiG/TiN5Y/a8YtIuzSA5y/SZZjP4TqoKDPq6uEejfJY6CMIllHbzkC2xOJbCTkdp+D
         J5VNDlu9DBJ32zVlggUzuMjTuMyLghmJ9JmihCs9lYTh4+XbIPEahtR+9lzxd6XD0c42
         aAIfOLL/yBFlvnllY/Ct4o8f5LrX5bHpT+5szcDqzAQnhwzybNdr6R423U2zrprPccf4
         4BnExw3lvYctldvzXohiCqxAX0UhXpxdLCVvhFTqcvkulH6T/BvX0QeualZo6LBAFkIf
         jUM7cs0YiLrZaIpc69ATR+RWq/D8DxmlpjVqr4RINwwfXFpC8G8LX2oUkB2oE8zbp84d
         JRpw==
X-Google-DKIM-Signature: v=1; a=rsa-sha256; c=relaxed/relaxed;
        d=1e100.net; s=20210112;
        h=x-gm-message-state:mime-version:from:date:message-id:subject:to;
        bh=mc57FoW6zrn7Wng6YTURYh5V8x/Z64llQvT+HxMvkRw=;
        b=k/6W4dIWzm0pGH9sOqVuzSQt9SPa9GXxRCo6kcs7+05/NMVZOW/oeulpF9EM7HvNnJ
         KA0A8jhT5b0mbHhC2ta7nxMiHNE+8C2hcJXl+HBqLhSmzZ2fqnlAsoWE35s9FLXlg7X+
         npjBTN7yCCnymmn9u5qlsjhRz9JW3zpAD4lLyB08milYaalOSVN4AnjU61cYCzs29p/f
         fuyFdyP0wwmPs40WzRjvIUR0Tdy+OLtfjZuBID8oKcSuuJogsjrOXfuvyjmZvnPh+jvd
         I/sb6wPpuY/aIbWwvUC57iH6CBHewlzlJTX9wKNQqyeatWTj6vEIURrEDlcjkkleT4Bv
         aSNg==
X-Gm-Message-State: AOAM531WYacP3xZNjjKbEWGrLDPqvP2mlXg2oixCMq05koiqoHbR4Kf4
        LtL4t5XXttneSuknglm0FHz4le/r77sMlkoA7J8wuH0bSU+2/g==
X-Google-Smtp-Source: ABdhPJy5+FeoruecJ4dhByNkBclOsZ2BgtEDN114QJTlpKkUk/4/PL0/xf/KV8j+eHcDG0Sr463FU9AvANlggAGZsoY=
X-Received: by 2002:a25:e0c7:0:b0:629:182a:4b75 with SMTP id
 x190-20020a25e0c7000000b00629182a4b75mr3770665ybg.539.1647506824642; Thu, 17
 Mar 2022 01:47:04 -0700 (PDT)
MIME-Version: 1.0
From: Nick Oles <phishingtestingdemo1@gmail.com>
Date: Thu, 17 Mar 2022 11:46:53 +0300
Message-ID: <CAGmvWOBSSUJAnC8o_3OU5mffBpO9mbbdGvY7VMc6Uc-gEQ4sZQ@mail.gmail.com>
Subject: This is a Test Email
To: phishingtestingdemo1@yahoo.com
Content-Type: multipart/alternative; boundary="000000000000c42e905da66131a"
Content-Length: 1047

--000000000000c42e905da66131a
Content-Type: text/plain; charset="UTF-8"

Hello,

This is a test email, I wonder how it got to my inbox?

Goodbye!

--000000000000c42e905da66131a
Content-Type: text/html; charset="UTF-8"
Content-Transfer-Encoding: quoted-printable

<div dir=3D"ltr"><div style=3D"font-size:14px"><font color=3D"#222222" face=
=3D"Roboto, RobotoDraft, Helvetica, Arial, sans-serif">Hello,</font></div><=
div style=3D"font-size:14px"><font color=3D"#222222" face=3D"Roboto, Roboto=
Draft, Helvetica, Arial, sans-serif"><br></font></div><div style=3D"font-si=
ze:14px"><font color=3D"#222222" face=3D"Roboto, RobotoDraft, Helvetica, Ar=
ial, sans-serif">This is a test email, I wonder how it got to my inbox?</fo=
nt></div><div style=3D"font-size:14px"><font color=3D"#222222" face=3D"Robo=
to, RobotoDraft, Helvetica, Arial, sans-serif"><br></font></div><div style=
=3D"font-size:14px"><font color=3D"#222222" face=3D"Roboto, RobotoDraft, He=
lvetica, Arial, sans-serif">Goodbye!</font></div></div>

--000000000000c42e905da66131a--
```

***Figure 1-7.*** *Raw email header in Yahoo!*

# Outlook Desktop Mail Application

The Microsoft Outlook desktop mail application regularly updates the interface, or appearance, of the mail application. For this reason, collecting the email header from the older application interface is covered first.

Once you have identified the email to examine, locate the File menu and select Properties, as shown in Figure 1-8.

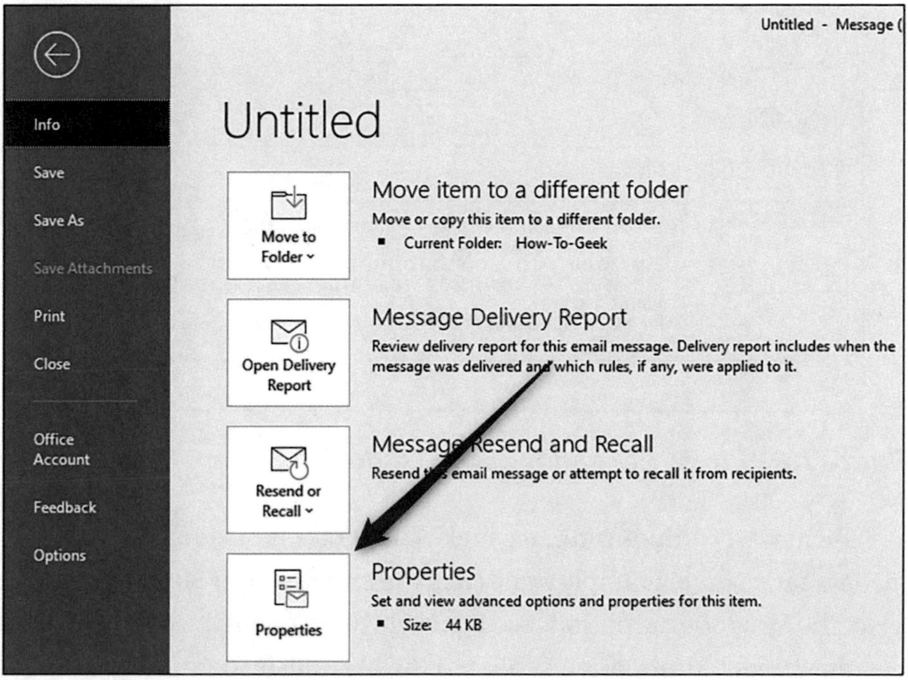


***Figure 1-8.*** *Outlook File menu*

The Properties dialog box appears, showing a box labeled Internet headers. This information can be copied, as depicted in Figure 1-9 (from howtogeek.com). Highlight all of the information in the Internet Headers box and press Ctrl+C on your keyboard to copy the data.

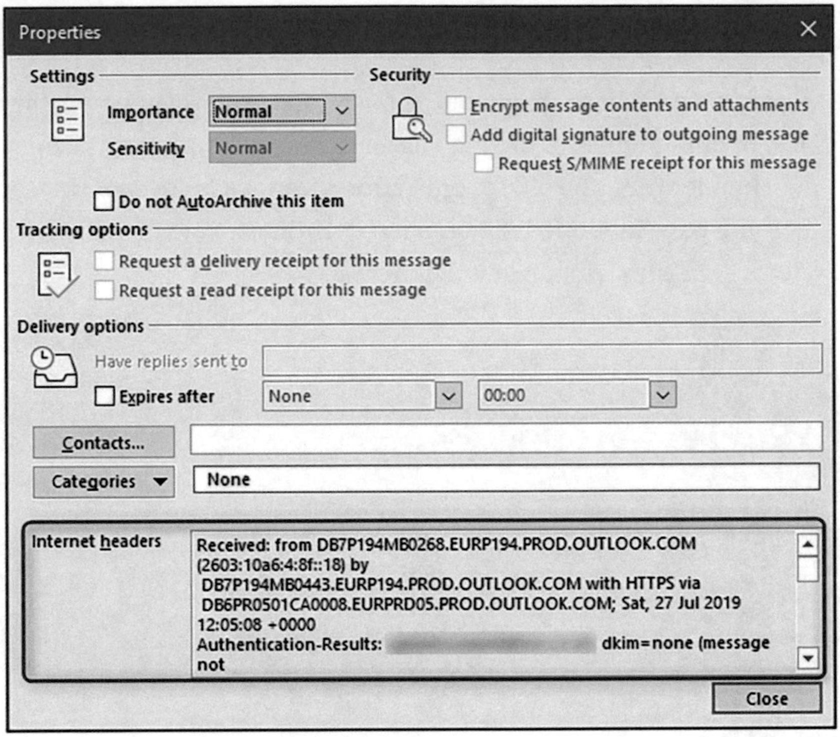


***Figure 1-9.** Properties dialog box in Outlook desktop application*

The newest Outlook interface makes the process of viewing email headers much easier. Simply right-click the email of your choosing and select the View Source option (see Figure 1-10). A dialog box appears with message header information similar to the previously identified processes.

***Figure 1-10.*** *Outlook email options*

You have now learned some options to view and collect email headers from three main email applications. A number of other mail applications exist, but covering each application would be exhausting and minimally useful. Instead, it is far better to understand the basic concepts and apply them to your specific mail application. Finally, it is important to understand that you must locate the mail header for the original message. A forward or reply to the message results in a new and vastly different email header. Always locate the original email and use it to examine the header information. It provides the most forensically sound and accurate information.

## Email Header Analysis Tools

As you have seen in previous examples, email headers are extremely data-rich. To help break out the pertinent information, a number of open source tools are available for free online. These tools do not alter the data but display the information more readably and effectively. Three of my favorite tools are MxToolbox, Google Admin Toolbox, and Microsoft Message Header Analyzer.

`https://toolbox.googleapps.com/apps/messageheader/`

`https://toolbox.googleapps.com/apps/main/`

`https://mha.azurewebsites.net/`.

## MxToolbox

The MxToolbox Email Header Analyzer is a mail vendor-agnostic tool that parses and reads headers from any mail client or application. It also offers several free and paid services to analyze IP addresses, domains, and email traits. Figure 1-11 shows the initial landing page at `https://mxtoolbox.com/Public/Tools/EmailHeaders.aspx`.

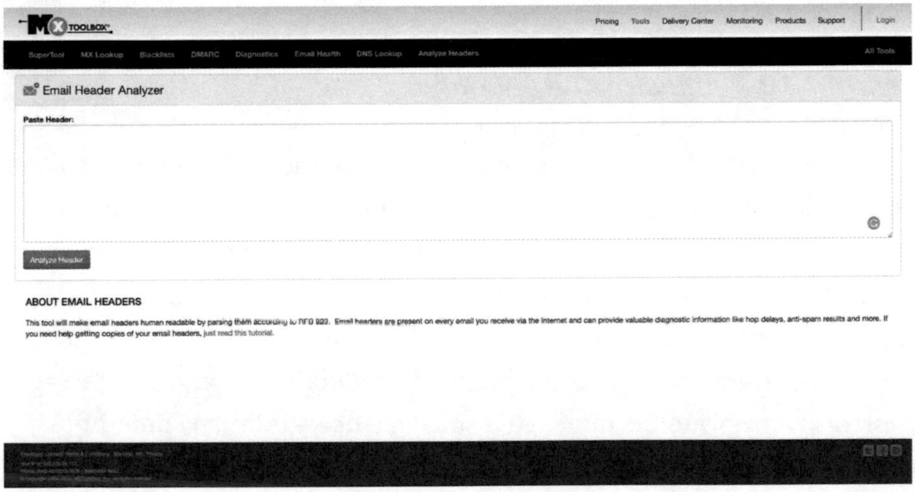


***Figure 1-11.*** *MxToolbox Email Header Analyzer*

Simply paste the raw header information into the dialog box and click the Analyze Header button. The page refreshes with a report showing the information analyzed from the raw header message. The information displayed is much easier to read and identify key details from the message.

Let's review each section, as shown in Figure 1-12, and highlight some of the relevant points.

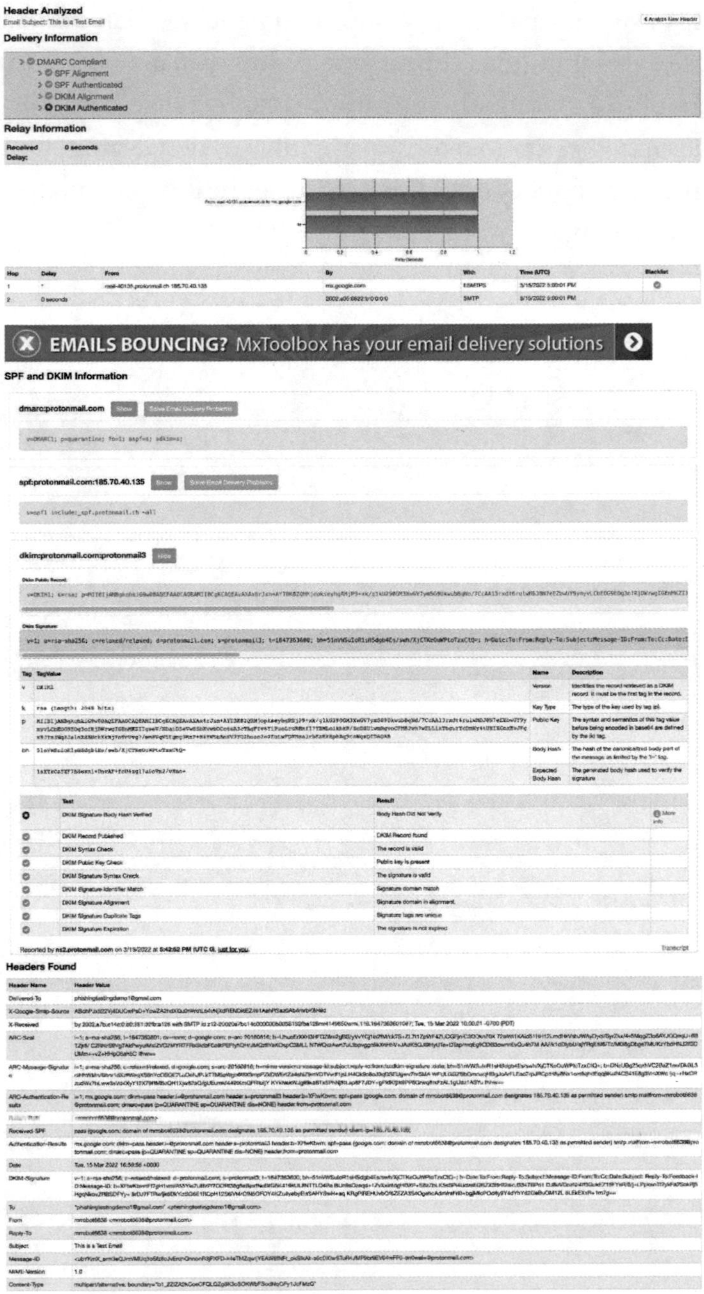


*Figure 1-12.* *Analyzed Message Header from MxToolbox*

- The **Header Analyzed** section covers the email subject provided from the raw email header. In our example, the subject is *This is a Test Email.*
- **Delivery Information** checks if the email is compliant with DMARC, SPF, and DKIM. These are email authentication methods organizations can use to validate authentication. Think of them as additional verification steps an organization has taken to show they are who they say they are.
- **Relay Information** shows the path the email message took. This is likely going to be SMTP servers and mail exchanges.
- **SPF and DKIM Information** offers additional specific information for the SPF and DKIM records.
- **Headers Found** is probably the most important section. It has Header Name and Header Value subsections. The following are a few fields of interest, which will be relevant in the coming chapters.
    - **Return-Path** is the email address that undeliverable messages are sent to. If the recipient address is invalid or unavailable, messages will be sent here.
    - **To** is the email address or addresses to which the email message was sent. Also known as the recipient.
    - **From** is the email address of the person who sent the message. It may be different than the address that appears in the message.

- **Reply-To** is the email address that receives replies from the original email. If you reply to a message, this is the address it goes to which can be different from the sender.
- **Received** shows a list of servers the message passed through with the associated IP or server name and the corresponding date and time. These servers are listed in reverse chronological order, meaning the first server is the last stop before being delivered. This section may also show the client's IP address used when the message was sent.

## Google Admin Toolbox

In some cases, you may want to use a message header analyzer specifically designed for a mail client or the sender's mail client. Specialized header analyzers can provide additional information and resources during your analysis. The Google Admin Toolbox is a great option for Gmail messages and works similarly to all other message header analyzers (see Figure 1-13). Start by collecting the raw header from the original message and pasting it in the text box.

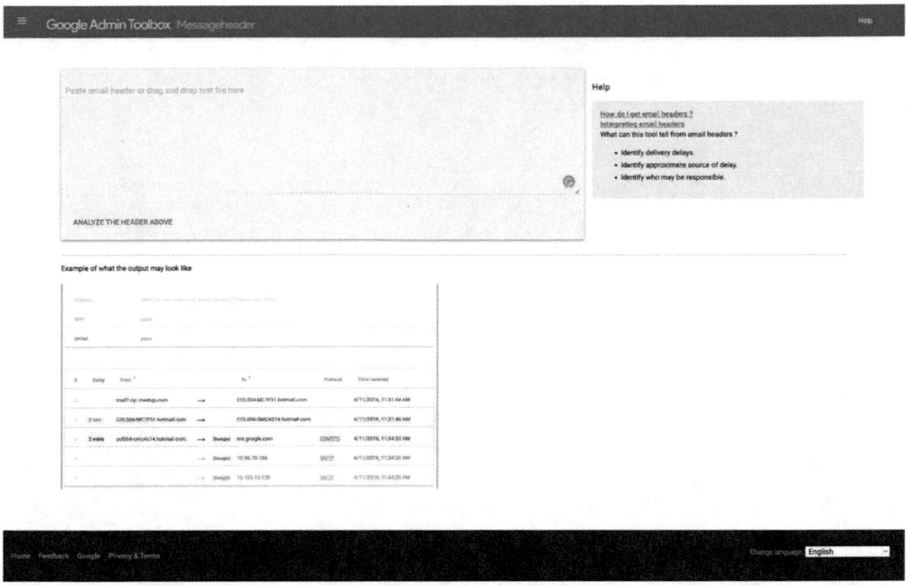


***Figure 1-13.*** *Google Admin Toolbox screenshot*

After providing the raw header information, the output shown in Figure 1-14 is received. The output varies vastly compared to the MxToolbox header analyzer. The top box shows basic message details and the compliance for email authentication. SPF, DKIM, and DMARC were mentioned previously. These are a set of email authentication methods used to validate to Internet service providers and mail services that senders are authorized to send mail from a particular domain. The specifics of each can get rather technical. It is important to know that they are for email validation. If any of these fail, it could be a sign of cause for greater concern. The second box shows the path the message took, starting with the Proton Mail server, moving to the Google mail exchange, and then two SMTP servers before delivery. It is important to note that the same header was used in both tools and provided different levels of summarized information.

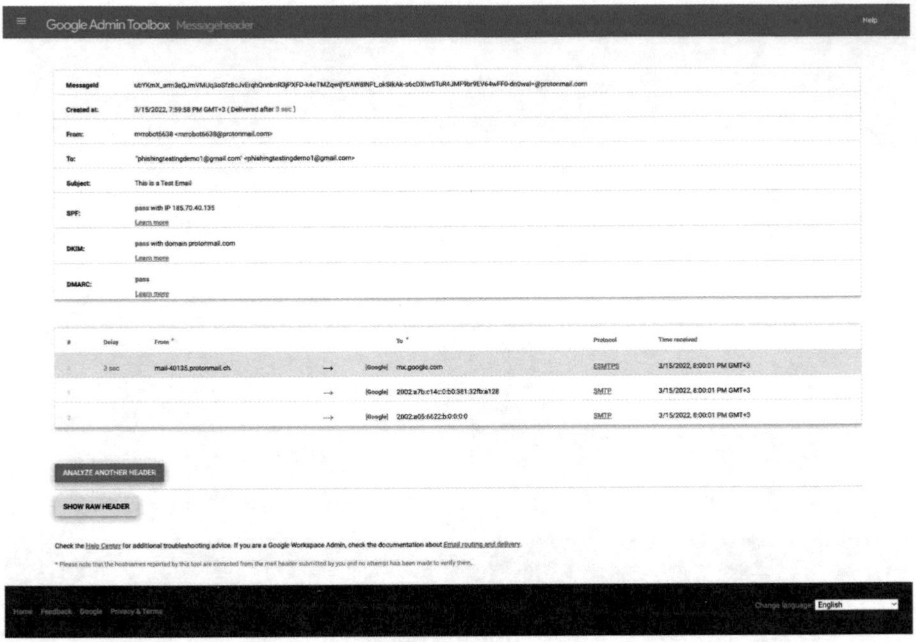


***Figure 1-14.*** *Google Admin Toolbox Messageheader*

# Microsoft Message Header Analyzer

The final tool covered is the Microsoft Message Header Analyzer. The header analyzer is geared towards Outlook messages and offers an interface and functionality similar to other header analyzers. Figure 1-15 shows a screenshot of the Microsoft Message Header Analyzer in action. Copy and paste the original raw message header into the dialog box and select the Analyze Headers button.

Once the message has been analyzed, the basic information is listed in the top section, followed by the route the message took, and finally, a chart with more detailed information. The output is similar to the MxToolbox analyzer.

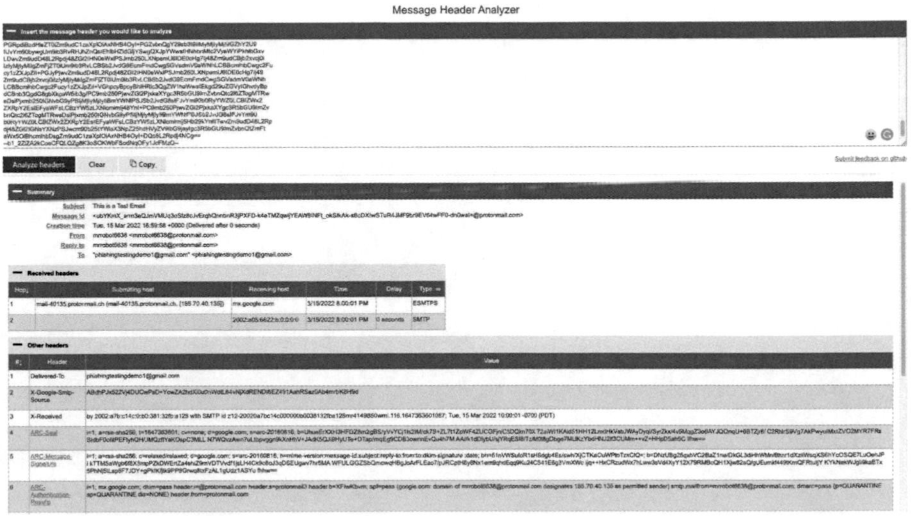


***Figure 1-15.*** *Microsoft Message Header Analyzer*

# Summary

This chapter discussed many of the technical details and topics regarding email. This information is crucial in beginning your journey investigating and identifying malicious email messages. Understanding the path and underlying technologies associated with a particular message aid in your adventures and thwarting activities. You explored how a message goes from a mail client through a series of servers and is delivered to its final destination anywhere in the world. The chapter also explained email headers, how to locate email headers on various mail platforms, and tools to help read and use the information stored in an email header. Now it is your turn to try analyzing email headers on your own; find some email messages and plug them into a few tools!

This chapter explained how email works, starting with the desktop or web application, through multiple servers, traversing the Internet, and being delivered to the intended recipient.

# CHAPTER 2

# Phishing Tactics and Techniques

Chapter 1 covered the basic components of email messages and headers. Now it is time to get into attack techniques. Attackers use techniques and tricks to entice end users to click a link, open an attachment, or send sensitive information unwittingly. Understanding these techniques helps you identify and scrutinize email messages that employ these or similar tactics. Before jumping into the nitty-gritty details, let's go over some of the basics.

Social engineering is the art of manipulating people to provide sensitive information or take a specific action. Art is an important word here, as this typically requires some soft skills and persuasion to achieve the desired results. The types of information sought varies, but the attackers usually try to trick you into providing sensitive information such as passwords or sensitive banking information, or attempt to access your computer secretly using installed malicious software. This software is often referred to as malware.

Social engineering is a technique that can be used both in person and remotely. In this book, I refer almost exclusively to the remote or digital use of social engineering. Figure 2-1 shows some of the main social engineering tactics.


N. Oles, *How to Catch a Phish*, https://doi.org/10.1007/978-1-4842-9361-4_2

***Figure 2-1.*** *Social Engineering Tactics (from antivirus software specialist Norton (us.norton.com)*

- Your "friend" sends you a strange message. This typically involves social media or email platforms. You have a previous contact or acquaintance that sends you a message that is out of character or context, such as a request for money, information, or to check out a link they are sharing with you. If this doesn't seem normal, it probably isn't, and your friend's account could be compromised. Contact your friend on a different mode of communication separate from the method that you were contacted on. For instance, if the initial message is an email, call your friend on a previously used or confirmed phone number.

- Your emotions are heightened. Attackers use fear, guilt, or sympathy as a catalyst in this approach, such as during a major disaster, pandemic, or incident. For instance, during the COVID-19 pandemic, attackers quickly created phishing campaigns related to the COVID-19 vaccine and related information or funds for assisting pandemic victims. They come in a variety of formats. Be cautious; if necessary, wait a few days to respond or act. In most cases, nothing is as urgent as it seems.
- The request is urgent. No one likes missing deadlines. Attackers use deadlines to make you think an action is needed immediately. It is commonly executed in password reset or account lockout-themed messages. The attacker's message claims an account is disabled, deleted, or reset if the user does not click a particular link.
- The offer feels too good to be true. Have you ever won the lottery without having bought a lottery ticket? This typically doesn't happen. Attackers often promise fame and fortune for completing a desired action. It could be the promise of a large sum of money if you first send a small amount, provide your banking information, or click a link to claim your prize. If it seems like your lucky day, it probably isn't.

- You're receiving help that you didn't ask for. This often comes in the form of technical support in which the attackers offer to fix a problem you didn't know existed. If you didn't request help, it's likely suspicious and potentially malicious. Verify the assisting party through a different mode of communication, like a phone call, before providing information.
- The sender can't prove their identity. If a message doesn't seem right and your attempts to verify the individual fail, it is likely a sign of malicious activity. It is better to be safe than sorry, and requesting additional information or verification is a safe and logical approach to dealing with these abnormal or unsolicited requests.

In addition to social engineering tactics, impersonation and account takeover are other common methods that attackers use. In impersonation, the attacker uses technology to appear that they are someone else, potentially a trusted third party. The attacker then uses the assumed identity to communicate, request information, or persuade a victim to click a link or interact with an attachment. Figure 2-2 shows a visual representation of impersonation.

***Figure 2-2.*** *Impersonation*

In an account takeover, the legitimate account of a user is compromised and used by the attacker. The attacker then uses the compromised account to target victims leveraging the compromised account's reputation. The FBI classifies this activity as Business Email Compromise (BEC) and claims it is "one of the most financially damaging online crimes."BEC attacks exploit the fact that many of us rely on email to conduct personal and professional business. Figure 2-3 from FBI.gov details the BEC process in four steps.

In a BEC scam, criminals send an email message that appears to come from a known or trusted source, making a legitimate request, like in the following examples.

- A vendor your company regularly deals with sends an invoice with an updated mailing address or account information.
- A company CEO or trusted senior executive asks an assistant or vender to wire money to a third party immediately.
- A homebuyer receives a message from his title company with instructions on how to wire his down payment.

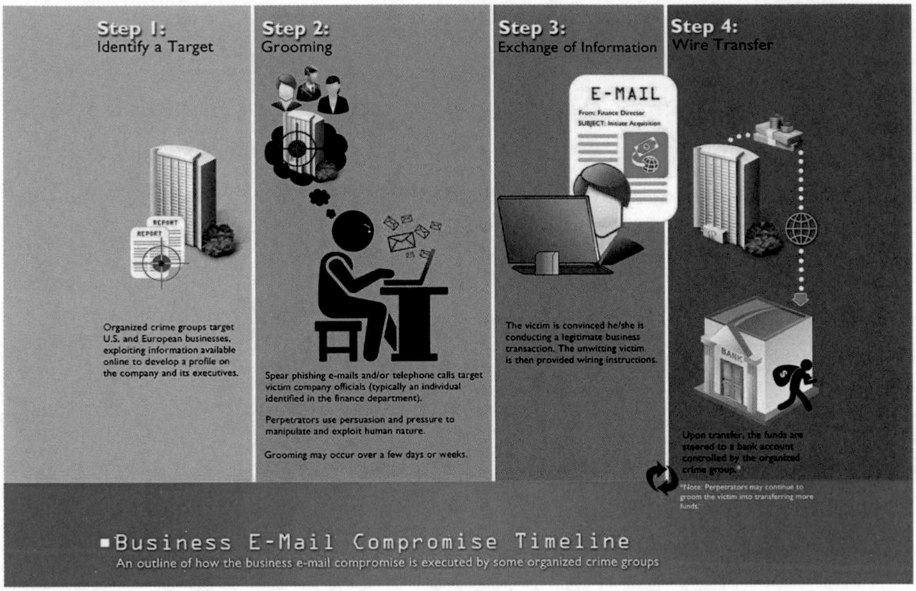


***Figure 2-3.*** *Business E-mail Compromise Timeline, FBI.gov*

Attack techniques and methods are developed and altered every day. No single, fully comprehensive list exists that can cover every possible scenario. These attacks have been continual and are rising in popularity. The methods explained can and are often combined to increase effectiveness. Visually inspecting and identifying suspicious traits is a critical step in catching a phish.

Figure 2-4 shows a message sent regarding a password reset for a university account.

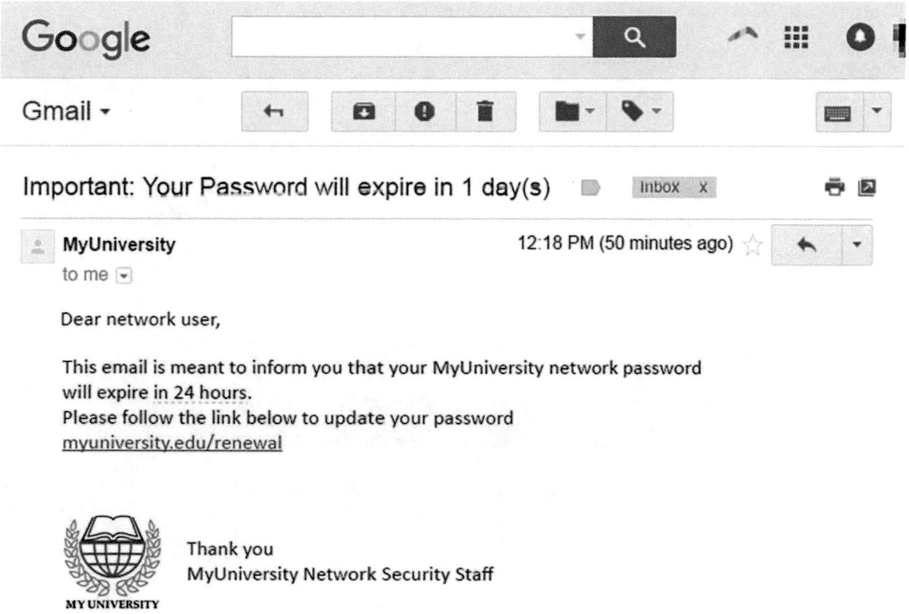


***Figure 2-4.** Suspicious message from imperva.com*

In Figure 2-4, you first read the subject and see it instantly portrays a sense of urgency and panic in the reader, stating their password will expire in one day. This instantly heightens our emotions and makes the request time-sensitive. The message contains a link that could be suspicious and uses a generic greeting instead of the recipient's name. Stay calm, don't click, we will examine this in more detail later.

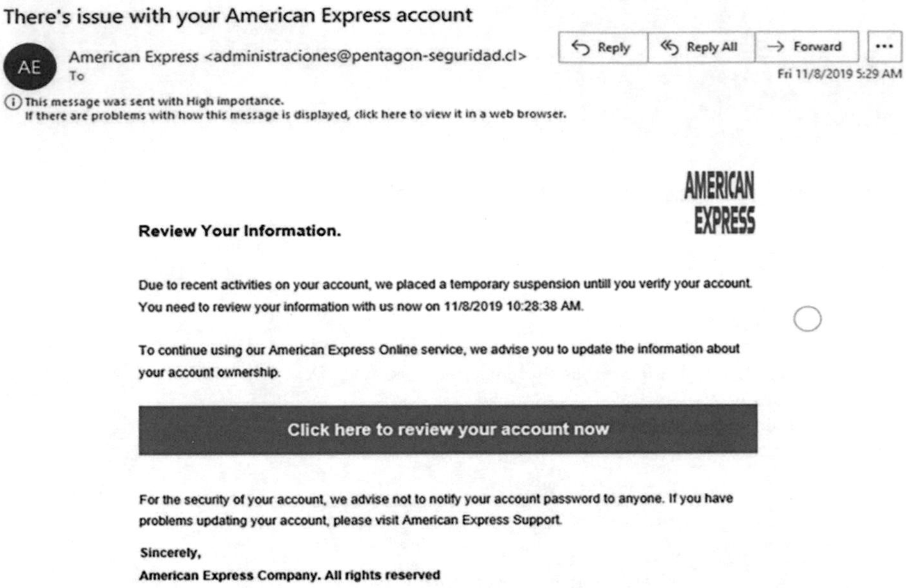


***Figure 2-5.*** *Suspicious banking message cheapsslsecurity.com*

In Figure 2-5 we review another suspicious that is banking themed. Building off the previous example, let's look at the subject and incorporate the sender's address. The subject conveys urgency and panic regarding an American Express account issue. Also, the sender address appears odd, coming from administraciones@pentagon-sguridad.cl. That does not appear to be an email address that your bank would use. Your "spidey senses" should be heightened at this point. Once you open the message, you see a logo that looks similar, but not identical, to the American Express logo. This is enough information to believe the sender is trying to impersonate or appear to be from American Express. The message informs you to click a button to review your account. This is the action the attackers are seeking.

# Summary

This chapter covered some of the many methods used by attackers. These techniques continue to change and evolve over time. The chapter also explored various attack techniques, defined social engineering, and provided some key indicators of suspicious messages to look out for. The coming chapters expand on these methods and identify ways to handle suspicious messages safely. This is an iterative process, which we continue to build on as you progress through this book!

# CHAPTER 3

# Incident Response

In addition to identifying suspicious messages, you need to have a plan to respond appropriately. Several frameworks or models exist to help support and lead the response efforts. The SANS organization has created and teaches one of the easiest and most relevant frameworks, PICERL, which is explained in this chapter. First, let's discuss some terms that help us better understand this framework and then we will dive into PICERL.

A *security incident* is an occurrence that jeopardizes the confidentiality, integrity, or availability of an information system. The incident can come in many shapes and sizes, but this book focuses on suspicious email messages. The messages are sent from attackers to victims, containing malicious links,attachments, or eliciting sensitive information. An attacker could compromise the system if a user interacts with a nefarious message.

*Incident response* is an organized approach to addressing and managing the aftermath of a security incident. It is the combined effort or actions taken to investigate, mitigate, and recover from an identified event.

*Malware* is software designed to disrupt, damage, or gain unauthorized access to a computer system. It is commonly delivered in malicious links or attachments through email messages. We previously referenced this as malicious software in a previous chapter.

An *incident response framework* is a process or procedure used to guide the response efforts of an incident. PICERL is near and dear to my heart and is my recommended response framework, although other frameworks exist and contain similar or overlapping information.


N. Oles, *How to Catch a Phish*, https://doi.org/10.1007/978-1-4842-9361-4_3

# PICERL

Sans.org is one of the world's leading cybersecurity training and certification organizations. It attracts some of the communities best and brightest researchers, students, and instructors. They created the PICERL process; and teach this incident response framework to students in several certification courses. Figure 3-1 depicts the six-step incident response process.

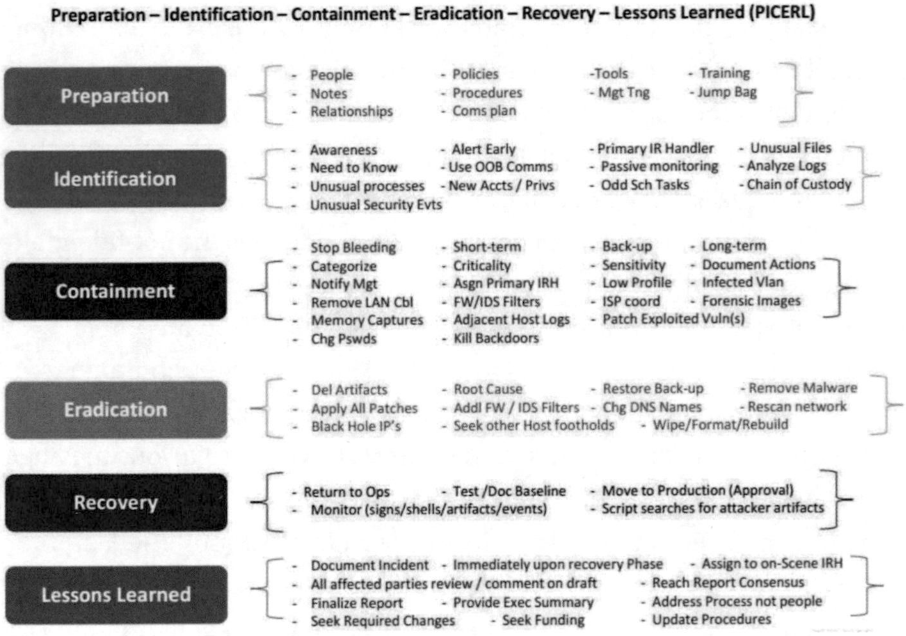


***Figure 3-1.*** *PICERL framework (Sans.org)*

Let's break down each phase and discuss how it applies to phishing emails and responses.

## Preparation

Preparation entails everything done before an incident occurred. These are the security controls you are using, any data you have proactively restored, and the plan you must execute if your machine becomes compromised. Users should back up sensitive data daily or weekly to minimize the impact of lost or compromised information systems. Ideally, data should be stored on two different media types, such as a USB drive and an external hard drive. The following cyber-hygiene recommendations help users minimize the impact of security incidents and recover faster.

- Use a reputable antivirus software and ensure it is updated regularly. Examples include Windows Defender, McAfee, Symantec, and Norton.
- Continuously update your operating system and installed applications. Most applications allow auto-update, this is a feature you should enable in most cases.
- Store and check copies of data regularly to ensure the data is relevant and usable. You should be able to restore data with little to no loss and quickly return to an operational state. Testing this will save you time and headaches.
- Think before you click, and be cautious when interacting with suspicious emails.
- Have a redundant or backup system if your primary information system is unavailable.

## Identification

Identification involves searching, documenting, and researching indicators of suspicious or malicious activity. Phishing messages focus on the sender, the body's content, and any links and attachments. These are all potential indicators or clues that could lead us to determine the message's validity. So far, you have explored some of these indicators, and the book continues expanding on them in the coming chapters. Let's review Figure 3-2 from Virginia.edu to understand this more. All of the circled and referenced points should be indicators of a suspicious message as they show signs of urgency, entice an action, or are suspicious in nature.

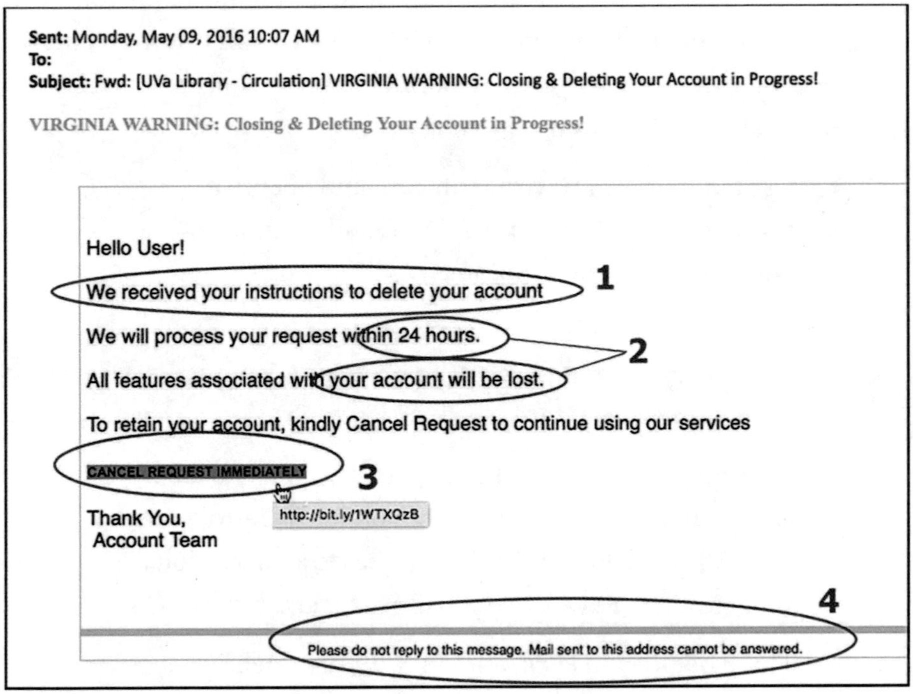


***Figure 3-2.*** *Virginia.edu suspicious email example*

## Containment

Containment involves isolating the impacted information system and preventing any further damage. You want to place the information system in a self-contained space to keep it from interacting or spreading to other systems. With phishing emails, you should immediately disconnect the machine from the wireless or wired network to stop or limit the spread to other devices on the network. If not done already, you would then begin to scrutinize the links and attachments you received in emails. You should run a full antivirus scan and ensure you are up to date with your operating system and installed applications. Figure 3-3 depicts a potentially infected machine being isolated and contained on the network.

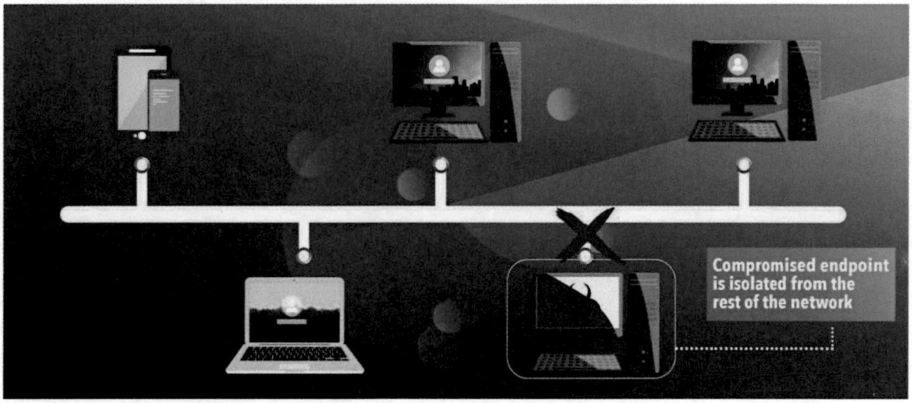


***Figure 3-3.*** *Containment (it-explained.com)*

# Eradication

Eradication removes the malicious software from the machine. Often this is done automatically by the antivirus program, but if not, you may need to remove the malware manually. In most cases, if malware is identified and cannot be removed using antivirus software, it is advised to reimage the laptop or restore it to its factory default settings. Any data stored on the laptop that was not backed up is likely lost. This is why daily and weekly backups are critical to minimizing a computer incident's impact.

The following are steps to eradicate malicious software from a machine.

1. Use antivirus or anti-malware software to remove malicious software. If your native antivirus software cannot remove the software, try using Malwarebytes or a similar application. Malwarebytes is one of the

top anti-malware removal tools and should be tried if unsuccessful proceed with steps 2 and 3.

2. Perform a factory reset of the PC. All data that is not stored offline or in the cloud is lost. The factory reset process is usually simple, with ample online instructions. Identify your operating system and research the most updated process for this using Google or your search engine of choice.

3. Attempt to reimage the machine using a fresh copy of the operating system.

## Recovery

Once you have identified and removed the malware, it is time to return our machine to a good, known working state. This entails installing all necessary software and ensuring the proper configurations are in place. You want to test your machine and confirm that you can do everything on the machine that you could do prior to the incident. You are putting the device back into full functionality, and now is the time to ensure things are set up correctly and safely. Figure 3-4 depicts a machine being restored to its good known state prior to the incident.

***Figure 3-4.*** *Recovery (Newyorkcomputerhelp.com)*

## Lessons Learned

The final phase of the incident response process is to identify ways to improve your system and incident response plan moving forward. You should identify what went well before, during, and after your incident. You should then identify what didn't go well and ways to improve. Examples might include restoring and testing your stored data monthly, reviewing emails closer, or switching to better antivirus software. The lessons learned section is intended to make this an iterative and self-improving process. See Figure 3-5 depicting the PICERL process in a flow chart.

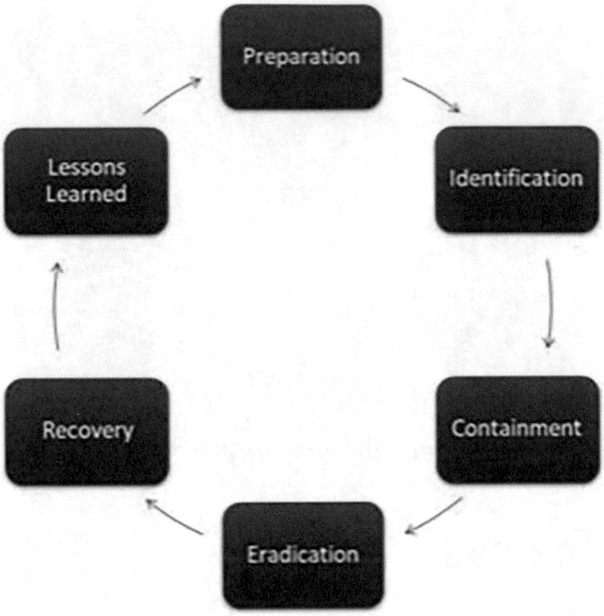


***Figure 3-5.*** *PICERL interative process*

# Summary

You learned about the PICERL process and how you can apply this to your environment while responding to security incidents. This iterative and extensible framework can be applied in any environment, regardless of size, including your home network or office environment. The process is intended to help guide you through responding to an incident. Your plan should be practiced and prepared before the incident occurs for the best results, which helps minimize the impact of an attack and quickly recover. The more time and thought put into your plan before the incident, the better chance that the results will be in your favor.

# CHAPTER 4

# Analyzing Message Content

*How* you say something is often far more important than *what* you say. This saying is relevant in our digital age as more human-to-human communication is moved from in-person to discussion using digital communication. The latest and greatest gadgets have given us the pleasure of carrying around supercomputers in each of our pockets capable of nearly any form of communication imaginable, including voice, data, video, and screen-sharing abilities. Attackers understand that more communication occurs in the digital realm and have looked at non-technical ways to persuade, illicit, and trick victims into providing sensitive information through message content. This chapter explains some of these techniques and how to identify things that don't seem right.

## What Is Content?

Before diving into all the details of how and why attackers craft messages the way they do, let's discuss the content of an email message. The information in the email message is typically written words, but sometimes images or symbols. It is how the sender of the message conveys information to the recipient. This comes in all shapes, sizes, and levels of


N. Oles, *How to Catch a Phish*, https://doi.org/10.1007/978-1-4842-9361-4_4

sophistication, but nearly all email messages have some form of content to convey information from one entity to another. Figure 4-1 shows an example of message content.

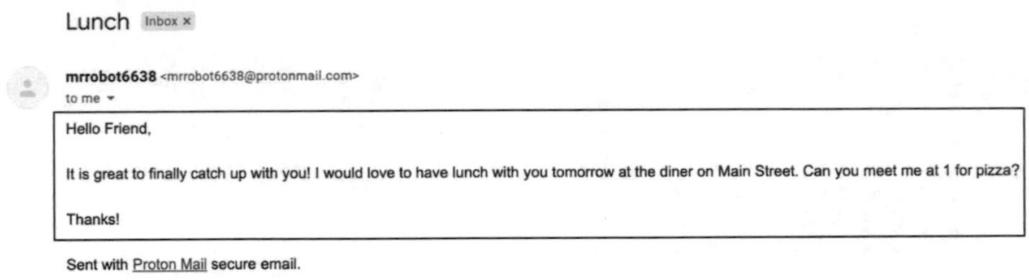


***Figure 4-1.*** *Example of written message content*

The highlighted box in red shows the message content from the sender to the recipient. By reading the content, you can see that the sender starts with a greeting to the recipient of *Hello Friend* and then requests a location and time for lunch. The sender finished the message with a simple closing stating *Thanks!*. The greeting and closing become more pertinent as you progress through the chapter. Right now, focus on understanding the content is the written information the sender provides to the recipient.

Text is not the only method to communicate an intended message via email. Many messages, frequently marketing related, contain images and graphics that convey the intended content. This can be as simple as an advertisement for your favorite movie, clothing brand, or sports drink. The advertiser could send a billboard-type message to the recipient to promote the product or service of their choosing. Clicking any portion of the image directs you to a website determined by the sender. This activity can be used for marketing or advertising purposes and nefarious activity. Figure 4-2 shows an example of a message containing a clickable image with some text built into the image.

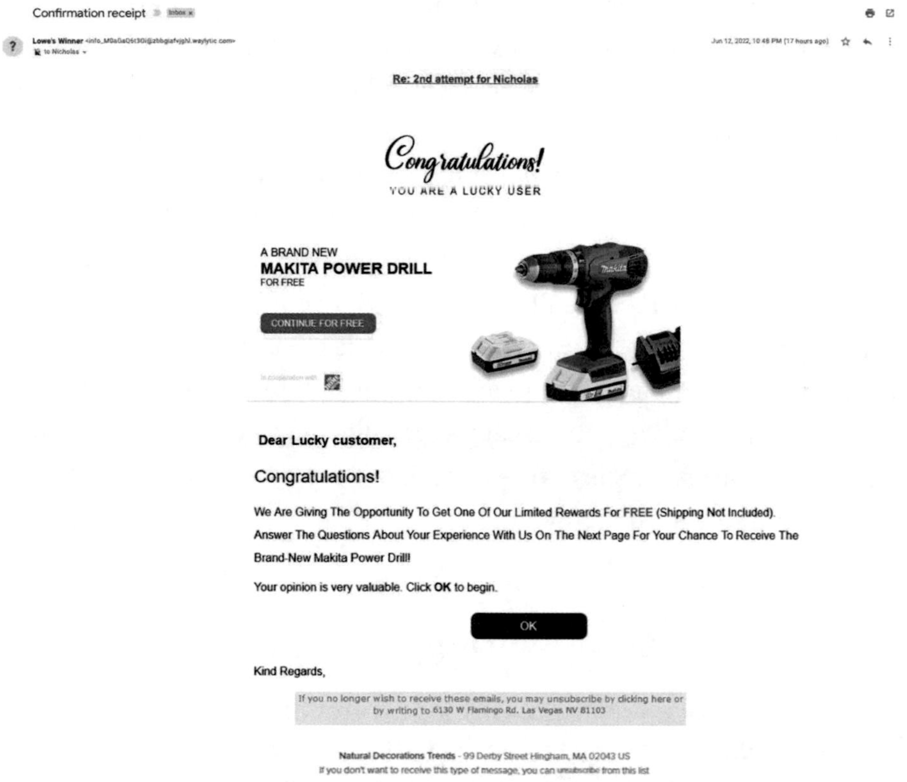


***Figure 4-2.*** *An image-based phishing message*

Now that you understand the basics of message content let's discuss how attackers use content to target victims. In most phishing campaigns, the attacker's desired outcome is for the victim to act. The attacker plans out his strategy much like a sports team or the coach plans out a game strategy. They first evaluate the intended audience learning as much as they can to help improve their odds of success. This information gathering process is often referred to as reconnaissance. They then evaluate the technologies and processes needed to create, deliver, and capitalize on the phishing message sent to the victim. This is often referred to as the actors infrastructure. Infrastructure can include many things, but to simplify, let's think of this as the tools the attacker needs to send the email, like a laptop, server, router, and switch. Once created and finalized, the attacker sends the message to entice the victim to complete the desired action.

Figure 4-3 explains *spear phishing*, a targeted attack toward a specific individual or user. This is very similar and often overlaps with the general concept of phishing. The key takeaway is that spear phishing is often very targeted and has a much smaller victim pool. In contrast, phishing can generally be sent to any number of individuals or sizes. For example, a spear phishing campaign might target five high-ranking individuals at a large company, and a phishing campaign might target 5,000 individuals in the same company. You can see by the numbers that one is much more targeted and specific than the other.

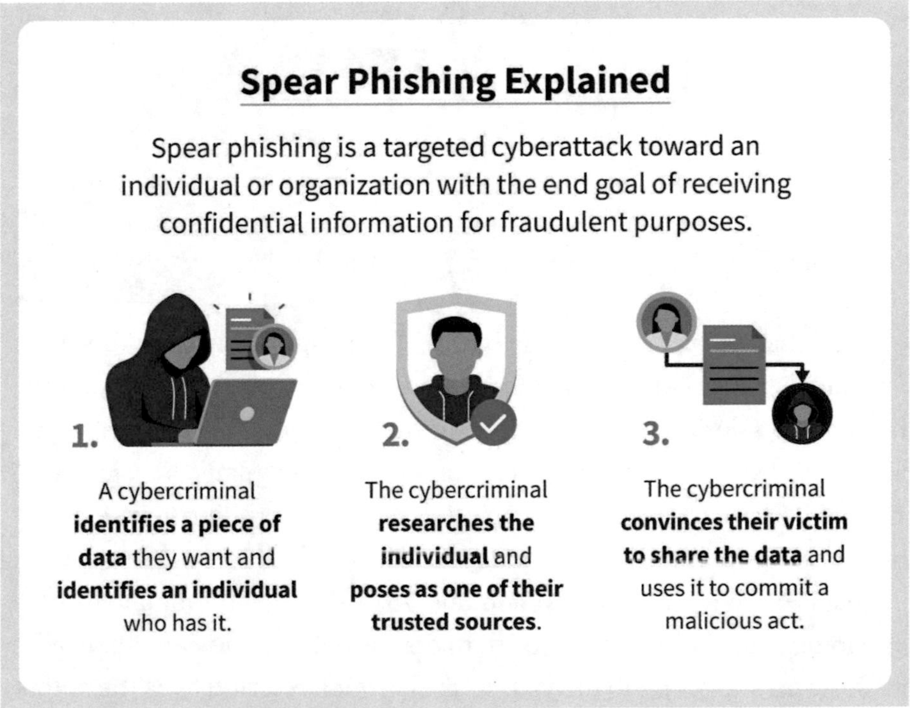


***Figure 4-3.*** *Spear phishing, as explained by Norton*

The way the attacker convinces the victim to click the link is often referred to as a tradecraft. They use this specific theme or process to convince the victim to click the link, download the attachment, or provide sensitive information. Each attacker takes a slightly different approach, but it is possible to identify these trends with enough time and resources. Using well-crafted content is the easiest and fastest way for an attacker to spin up a campaign. This requires very little technology or infrastructure setup to send a convincing email. These are often the hardest emails to detect with modern security tools and technologies that focus on link analysis and email attachment scanning.

The best way to defend against these attacks is through training. To aid in the training value, look at some phishing emails, such as Figure 4-4, and review each message's suspicious components. This habit becomes more natural with practice and time, and soon you are catching phishing emails on your own without even realizing it!

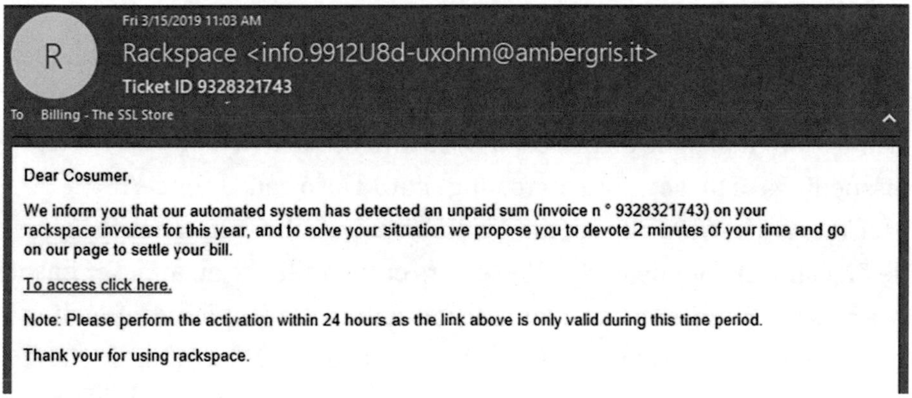


***Figure 4-4.*** *A sample phishing email, thesslstore.com*

Figure 4-4 shows an email message sent from one email account to another. The content of the message looks to be an automated email regarding an invoice. The sender appears to be from an organization or person named Rackspace, which happens to be a large information technology organization that specializes in data storage. The message is asking for payment of an overdue invoice with a link provided to pay the outstanding balance. Does anything look suspicious?

This section ignores the email sender and recipient. The first part of the email starts with a greeting from the sender to the recipient. This particular message starts with **Dear Cosumer,**. Analyzing this greeting tells you a few things. First, the sender made a mistake and misspelled the word *Consumer*. This is suspicious but not uncommon; every one of us has sent an email with a grammatical error. What is more interesting is that the sender sent this very generic greeting. You don't see a name or account information, just the words *Dear Consumer* with a spelling error.

## Message Greetings

Attackers often use these types of generic greetings to reach a larger audience without needing customization. Greetings such as Valued Vustomer, Friend, Dear Account Holder, Hi Dear, and other variations should all alert you that this greeting is not specific to you and therefore has the potential to be an indicator of suspicious activity. Furthermore, misspellings of these or other greetings could also cause concern. Attackers are located all over the world, and English is often not always the first spoken language. Spelling errors could indicate an attacker hastily writing a phishing email and sending it out without proper proofreading. These are both signs of potential suspicious activity. None of them should be used as sole sources for identification, but rather a series of clues with other factors that can aid you in your determination.

Next, let's look at the body of the message. The message says you have an unpaid balance. To solve this situation, you must click the provided link to settle your bill. The link is only good for 24 hours, insinuating that you only have a short period of time to take action. The content of this message is inciting a sense of urgency and action for the recipient. A past-due account and a link to remediate the issue within only 24 hours puts the reader on edge. Seeing all these things makes the reader think they must act quickly to fix this problem or face some adverse action. This is a good example of inciting urgency and eliciting the action of clicking a specified link.

## Threatening or Urgent Requests

Another tactic commonly used by attackers using specifically crafted content is to make threatening or urgent requests that result in adverse actions. The actors want you to ignore all indicators that a message is suspicious and instead focus on the adverse action that occurs if you fail to comply with their request. This scare tactic continues to work on victims across many industries and platforms.

Figure 4-5 is a well-crafted threatening email request. The message is supposedly sent from McAfee, a leading antivirus and cybersecurity organization with decades of experience in the industry. Some might call them an OG, or original gangster, meaning they have been in this game for a long time.

Let's start at the top of the message and work our way down. This is typically a logical and easy-to-follow approach to reviewing messages for indicators. The top of the message is enhanced to make things easier to read. The message starts with the subject *Confirmation Receipt*. This subject was selected to make the reader think they recently purchased this product. It is a good hook to get the reader to open the email to review the receipt and see what they purchased. This should be your first suspicious indicator if you didn't purchase anything, specifically from McAfee, or don't have any McAfee products.

Next, look at the sender of the message. At first glance, it might appear that the sender is McafeeRenewal, but if you look closer, you see the email address is vastly different. This message appears to come from info_M0aGsQ1nu54@xypkathgtvpg.waylytic.com. A few things are going on here. First, the sender is trying to appear as if the message is coming from McAfee by displaying the name McafeeRenewal. However, the attackers did a poor job of masking the sender address, and the mail application rendered a different sender address. This could have also been determined using email header analyzer tools that we discussed in previous chapters.

The sender's address looks suspicious at best and likely malicious. It contains several letters and numbers that appear to be thrown together randomly. The domain, which is everything after the @ symbol, is almost unreadable. When reviewing the sender's message, you want to ask if this looks like something the sender should be using as a valid email address. For example, someone working at McAfee likely has an email address that ends in @mcafee.com, like nick@mcafee.com. I wouldn't expect any legitimate organization to use the domain xypkathgtvpg.waylytic.com. Would you?

*Figure 4-5.* *Sample phishing email*

After reviewing the subject and sender address of the message, let's now look at the content in the body of the email. The top of the email contains a hyperlink informing you it's your "final notice" on your McAfee subscription expiring. They are nice enough to tell us that our devices will no longer be protected. No one wants to have expired licenses or unprotected devices. As you continue reviewing the content of the message, you see a photo of a smiling woman using her laptop and a limited offer for a 50% discount on McAfee Antivirus. This deal is too good to be true. How could you ever pass this up?

Did you pick up any these or other indicators while reviewing the content of this message? If so, what were they? Below are some points to consider.

The initial line is an urgent request that results in our devices no longer being protected if you do not take immediate action. This claims to be our final notice, but did you get any notices before this? Do you use this product at home or in the office? If the answer is no, add these to your list of growing indicators regarding the validity of this message. You see the woman smiling at her laptop in the photo. Images like this are often used in the message to entice or further distract the recipient. We close out the content with a lucrative offer to save 50% on purchasing the software and a large red button to redeem this offer. Looking at the totality of the indicators identified, this message would be suspicious at best and likely malicious, as it uses urgency and adverse activities occurring if an action is not taken.

# Impersonation Attempts

Attackers often impersonate or mask their identity to appear as someone they are not, as a figure of authority or a trusted party to achieve a desired action. Research is conducted before the attack to determine the ideal individual to impersonate and potential targets to send messages to. Often, the attackers impersonate a person with prestige and power within an organization, such as the chief executive officer (CEO), chief financial officer (CFO), or, my favorite, the chief information security officer (CISO). The attacker attempts to make the message look like it is sent from a figure of authority and is received by a subordinate in the organization. Victims often feel empowered or fear repercussions if they do not take the desired action. It could be interpreted that reporting or ignoring these emails might result in disciplinary action.

Look at Figure 4-6 and use a top-down approach to review the message. Start with the message's subject, which asks, *Are You Free?*. This is a generic subject, but at this time does not raise any imminent questions or causes for concern. Start with the sender and recipient addresses. The sender here is mrrobot6638@protonmail.com, which could be suspicious or expected. Note this for now and continue working through the email.

***Figure 4-6.*** *Impersonation email*

Next, look at the greeting and content of the message. The greeting used in this message is a basic *Hello Tim*. You see that the sender is using the recipient's first name, which could be a sign that they trust, respect, and know this person well enough to use the individual's first name in the greeting. It might be a sign of rapport or verification that the sender knows who they are talking to. When you get to the content body, the sender states they are in a meeting and have an urgent request asking for a response as soon as possible. The signature says the message is from John Smith, the CEO of Mr. Robot Corp.

Now that you've read the entire message, let's work through what was identified and discuss potential suspicious indicators. First is the subject, no apparent signs of suspicious activity in the subject by itself. The sender claims to be the CEO of Mr. Robot Corp. Usually, you would expect the email to come from someone like John@mrrobot.com or CEO@mrrobot.com. This sender's address is suspicious, but by itself is not enough for us to stamp this email as malicious. If you look at the content, the sender claims to be in a meeting and needs you to respond as soon as possible. Is this normal activity? Does the CEO regularly email you during meetings with immediate requests? Possibly, but in most cases, probably not. The recipient would have to evaluate the totality of the circumstances and determine if this is normal. In most cases, the CEO is not making this request, which is the start of an impersonation attack. The attacker typically asks the recipient to purchase gift cards, money orders, or to send money in some other form to the CEO quickly while they are still in a time sensitive meeting. The employee often oblige to avoid letting down the CEO or in hopes of earning some brownie points with the company's leadership.

Multiple indicators lead us to believe that messages are suspicious or likely malicious. To analyze email message content effectively, it is important to review the email slowly and understand what the sender asks you and the details surrounding the request. Does this make sense? Is this something the sender should be requesting of me? Are there any specific flags or areas of concern? Have I reviewed this email from top to bottom to understand the full context and indicators that might exist? Answering these questions and using the tips covered in this chapter and others help you determine if the message is valid and how to proceed.

## Summary

This chapter dove deep into message content and how attackers can use it to trick you. It explained spear phishing and different methods attackers use to quickly establish credibility and entice a recipient to act. This information should help you pick up on additional suspicious indicators as you continue learning and improving your “Spidey senses”.

CHAPTER 5

# All About Links

So far, this book has discussed many of the components of an email message and some indicators that can help us determine the validity of a message. The last chapter focused on content and various ways that content can be used as an attack method. Email messages can contain far more than just content. Often, messages are sent with links or attachments to help convey additional information to support the content in the main body. This chapter focuses on links and how attackers use them to exploit and attack victims.

## What Is a Link?

A link is short for *hyperlink* and refers to a data point. The data point is usually a website, but it can also point to files, folders, or documents stored locally on the network or workstation. For phishing and email purposes, most links are associated with websites. The website contains content that is created and maintained by the website owner. This content can cover any topic desired and contain various forms of data such as text, audio, software code, or video. The content is created, stored, and modified on a web server. Let's pause here and help explain this a little better with an example.

Mr. Nick wants to create a website detailing the latest cybersecurity news articles he reads daily. Once he comes up with this idea, he must determine how he shares it with his intended audience. He decides that a website is the best way to attract and share content with his fellow nerds.


N. Oles, *How to Catch a Phish*, https://doi.org/10.1007/978-1-4842-9361-4_5

(Think *computer enthusiast* if the word *nerd* offends you.) Mr. Nick has two options for storing his content. He can buy and manage his own web server or rent one from a company. Mr. Nick decides to rent a server from a company, as it is cheaper, easier, and faster than managing his own. Once the server is up and running, he can start creating his content.

Next, Mr. Nick needs to make his web server accessible to the Internet through an Internet Service Provider (ISP). Everyone with an Internet connection has dealt with an ISP. An Internet connection allows you to create and publish content. Mr. Nick finds a website-hosting platform where he can quickly create and publish content. For most sites, this free or cheap platform, such as WordPress, allows users to create and publish content in minutes with little technical knowledge and no development needed. Platforms like WordPress let you publish the site through their domains for free, but many serious content creators register their own domains.

Finally, Mr. Nick is super savvy and needs to register a domain for his new site. The domain is the website's name; it is used to find the content Mr. Nick publishes. Examples of domains include cnn.com, yahoo.com, and espn.com. Domains are registered through a domain registrar, which is an organization that buys and sells domain names. Typically domains are purchased for one to three years with the option to renew if desired. The domain is very important for people to remember and recognize your page. Once you've created the content, domain, and platform, you can share hyperlinks directing people to your site. Again, the hyperlink is simply the pointer or reference to a resource; in this case, it would be your web page.

## Links in Emails

Email messages are sent at an alarming rate across the Internet, with some resources estimating nearly 300 billion emails are sent each day. Many of these emails are marketing and advertising; a small percentage of the overall messages are used for legitimate email purposes. Links often accompany email messages to help direct the end user to a resource typically related to the email content. Email links are embedded into the content of the email message. Chapter 4 discussed content, and the links can be stored in various locations. Attackers can add links to message content in various locations to entice the recipient to click the message and visit an intended page.

Let's look at a few examples of embedded links in the coming figures. Figure 5-1 shows a full-size image of a delivered phishing email, followed by a zoomed-in picture of the message content.

*Figure 5-1.* *A link in a phishing email*

***Figure 5-1.*** *(continued)*

As you scan through this message from top to bottom, you can start to evaluate this message for suspicious indicators. Let's focus on the links within the message. The very top of the message contains a hyperlink named *Nicholas Camp Lejune Justice Act of 2022 - New Claims*. The senders have inputted the first name of the intended recipient and a bogus government act that appears to be new, all inciting the recipient to review this message closer and click something sooner rather than later. As explained in Chapter 4, the personalized greeting is a way to build rapport and convey trust quickly with the recipient. This should have raised a few flags initially.

Continuing down the message content, you are greeted with the word *ATTENTION* in large block text. The image then conveys information regarding one million military and civilian staff being compensated for contaminated drinking water. The image ends with a WHAT'S MY CLAIM WORTH? button. What the reader can't see is that in addition to the hyperlink at the top of the email and the button at the bottom of the email, the entire image is a hyperlink. Clicking anywhere in the image direct the recipient to the sender's intended resource. Attackers use this little trick to increase the odds of the recipient clicking the message potentially in error or purposefully. The end user might not be aware that the image itself contains a hyperlink. This is why it is especially important to interact with suspicious messages with caution. It is a good practice to use the scroll bar or down arrow when examining an email in question to avoid accidental clicking.

Let's now discuss the footer, which is the end portion of an email message. This typically contains two sections. The first is the ability to unsubscribe or remove the recipient's address from the mailing list or preferences that the company used to send the message. The unsubscribe button or feature can sometimes work by removing the recipient from the list. But, attackers have caught onto this feature and can use the unsubscribe link as a final attempt to dupe the recipient into clicking a malicious link. Be cautious with interacting with the unsubscribe link. Blocking the recipient or closely examining the link before clicking it is typically preferred. Figure 5-2 enhances the message, focusing on the footer.

The final section in this and many emails contain the sending organization's contact information. In Figure 5-2 you see an address and yet another link to stop incoming messages from being delivered. This is oddly similar to the unsubscribe link provided and is commonly used by attackers to insert a link in another section of the message. The bottom line is that links in any part of the message can be malicious. They are strategically placed throughout the content and disguised as a multitude of things used to obscure their intended purpose.

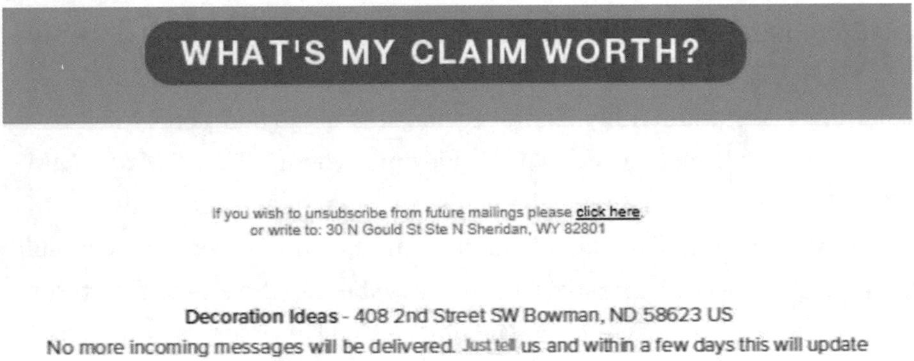


***Figure 5-2.*** *A footer in a message*

Another method of using embedded links is to focus less on images and more on the written content to entice the end user. Figure 5-3 also uses embedded links to entice the recipient to click an intended hyperlink. Take a few minutes to examine the email from top to bottom.

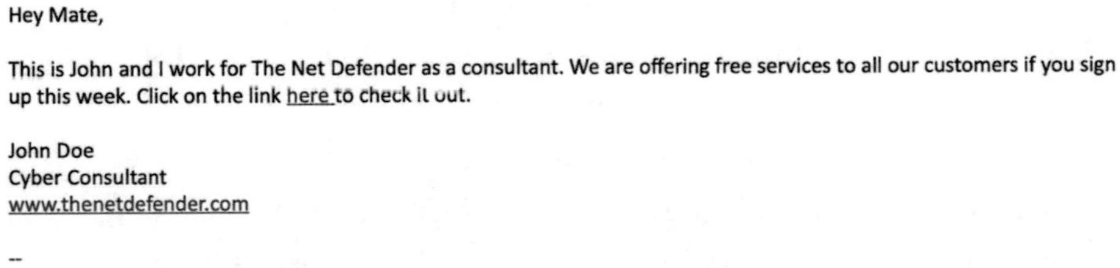


***Figure 5-3.*** *Embedded links in email*

Let's start by reviewing the message from top to bottom, disregarding the sender, recipient, and subject for this exercise. The message starts with a greeting using an informal nickname or greeting. Although slightly different than using the first name, it still conveys a sense of rapport and trust. The sender is offering services free for a limited time. A link is provided, followed by the signature of the sender. The sender has communicated an offer that incites action with the hope that the user clicks the hyperlink.

## What to Do

Unfortunately, attackers have continued to embed malicious links in emails for many years. This technique is quite effective and continues to have a rapidly increasing pool of potential victims. Several hardware and software solutions exist to scan emails for malicious links, but these are typically only feasible in corporate offices. For everyday end users like you and me, the best risk mitigation method for these attacks is through training and vigilance. To further help detect malicious activity, you need to examine links manually or with tools. If you are not tech-savvy—fear not, we will walk through this process slowly, and it is something any email user can do.

## Link Hovering

One of the easiest approaches to reviewing a link for validity before clicking is to hover over the link. This simple method typically displays the website or resource the hyperlink points to. The key here is to review the resource the link is directing you to and ensure that it coincides with the supporting content. For instance, a hardware store sends an email to potential or previous customers regarding a sale of lumber. The email contains a link to the hardware store website with the sale details. So far, nothing in this theorteical message appears abnormal or suspicious, but being a computer enthusiast, you want to review the link before clicking. You simply hover your mouse slowly over the link and review the intended resource that it is pointing to. You expect to see a domain or resource that aligns with the hardware store, like the name of the hardware store. If you see a domain name or resource that isn't related to the hardware store or lumber, it could indicate a malicious message. It is important to do this before clicking, as once the link is clicked, your computer starts its journey to the intended resource, which could result in a malicious page or code.

Figure 5-4 shows an example of link hoving.

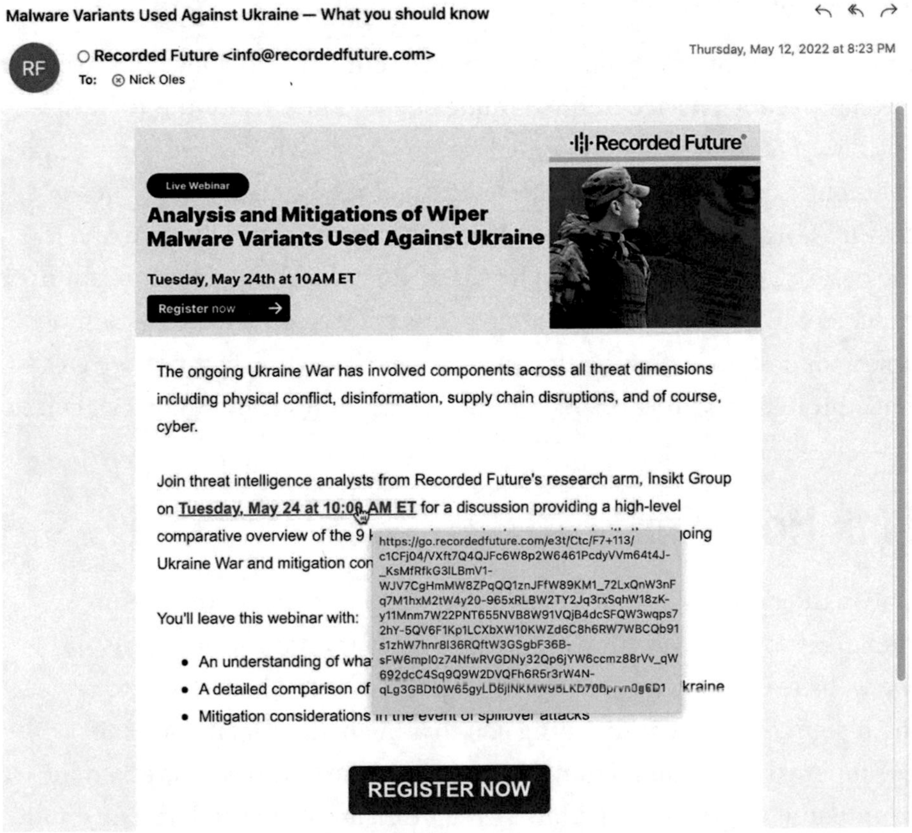


***Figure 5-4.*** *Benign link hovering*

The email in Figure 5-4 references a webinar with a link to register to attend. By simply placing the mouse on the hyperlink, the preview feature of the browser or mail application should provide the intended resource. It is important to note that we did not click the link, we placed the pointer over the link. Some browsers or mail applications may not have this setting turned on or enabled, but at this time, most do. While reviewing the link details in Figure 5-4, it appears to go to the organization's website that sent the email. It would not raise any immediate flags at this time.

Unfortunately, links do not always direct to a safe resource. In Figure 5-5, hovering over the link reveals a message with suspected malicious intentions. The short message offers a deal for free services. The sender mentions The Net Defender organization and links to its website in the signature block. You would presume that the *here* link in the email would direct you to The Net Defender website or something similar. Instead, it takes you to `www.thisisaviruspleaseclickhere.com.ru.cn`. It looks nothing like what you expected and is a strong indicator of malicious activity.

***Figure 5-5.*** *Link hovering shows malicious indicator*

Now that you understand link hovering make it a part of your review routine. You are learning additional tips and tricks to help improve your email evaluation process. The good news is that the more you do this, the better you become. The bad news is link hovering sometimes isn't enough. Sometimes it is necessary to extract the link and use additional tools to check the site's validity. Doing this may sound advanced, but anyone can safely analyze embedded links with a few free tools and a working mouse.

# Link Extraction

A computer mouse is the first and potentially most important link extraction tool. Every computer has a mouse ( an input device) that allows the user to navigate a pointer throughout the monitor. You can use your finger on the touchpad or display screen to act as a mouse for laptops or tablets. For desktops and laptops, it is typically more common for the user to have a physical hardware mouse that connects to the computer using the universal serial bus (USB). For effective link extraction, it is strongly recommended that you purchase a mouse if you do not have one natively. Extracting links can be done without a hardware mouse, but it is much easier and lessens your odds of clicking a suspicious link in error. They cost less than $20 online or in any retail store with an electronics section.

The mouse can come with bells and whistles, but you are concerned with only two buttons. They are the right-click and left-click buttons. Figure 5-6 shows a graphic of a mouse depicting the left and right mouse click buttons. The left-click button is the default to click, select, or highlight an object with the pointer. The left-click is what you use every day on your computer. Clicking a hyperlink with the left-click button takes you to the intended resource. The right-click provides additional functionality, often in drop-down menus or additional options. Clicking a hyperlink with the right-click button in an email presents additional options but does not direct you to the intended resource. This is very important to know when extracting links.

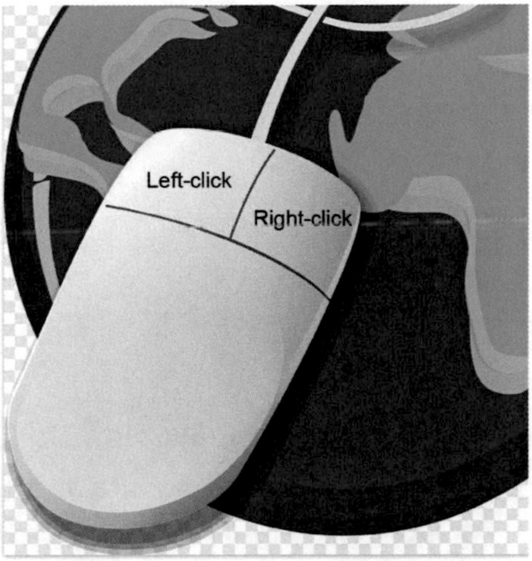


***Figure 5-6.*** *Mouse left- and right-click buttons*

Figure 5-7 uses the right-click button on the mouse to click the link. Again to stress these very important points, if you use the left-click button, you visit the intended resource, which could be malicious. To extract links safely, you must use the right-click button for the additional menu options and features. The example shows that the option to copy the link appears at the top of the menu box, which is precisely what you want to do for link extraction. You are attempting to copy the link to review it in a safe environment. You do not want to visit the link if you are unsure of its validity until you can further research and decide on its validity. Select the Copy Link option at the top of the menu bar to copy the link.

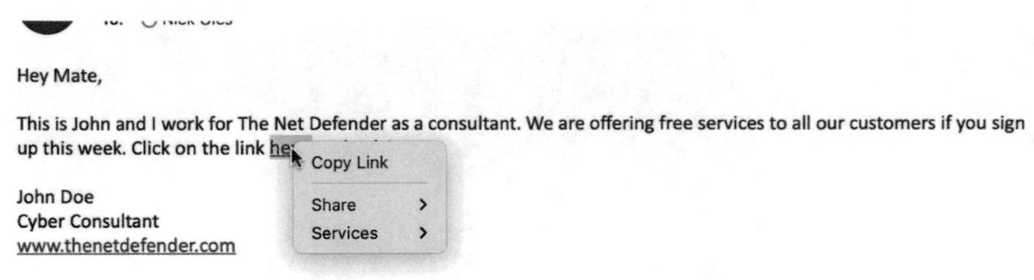


***Figure 5-7.*** *Mouse right-click*

What to do with the copied link now? Wouldn't it be swell to view the page on the link or see if others identified the site as malicious? This can be done in seconds with just a few more mouse clicks. The best part is all of the tools needed for this are also free and readily available to anyone on the Internet.

# VirusTotal

VirusTotal (`www.virustotal.com`) analyzes links and attachments to detect malicious software and content. It leverages information from over 94 different antivirus and security companies. The number of security organizations that participate changes, so this ebb and flow over time. Once a link is provided, VirusTotal scans the page and checks to see if any security vendors have classified the page as malicious or benign. It also features a community option for users to comment or discuss a site or malware sample. Figure 5-8 shows the landing page of VirusTotal and the sample URL.

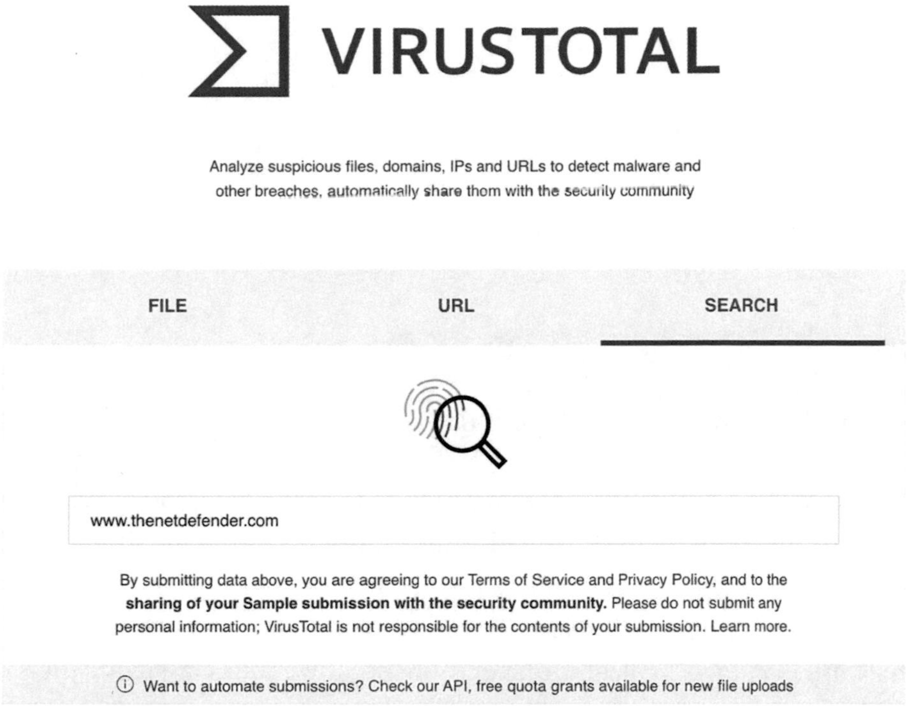


***Figure 5-8.*** *VirusTotal link submission page*

You simply need to right-click the search box and select paste. You then click the search button to begin the page analysis. The results return rather quickly, displaying any known matches for malicious activity based on the security vendors. Figure 5-9 shows the link submitted had zero signs of malicious activity.

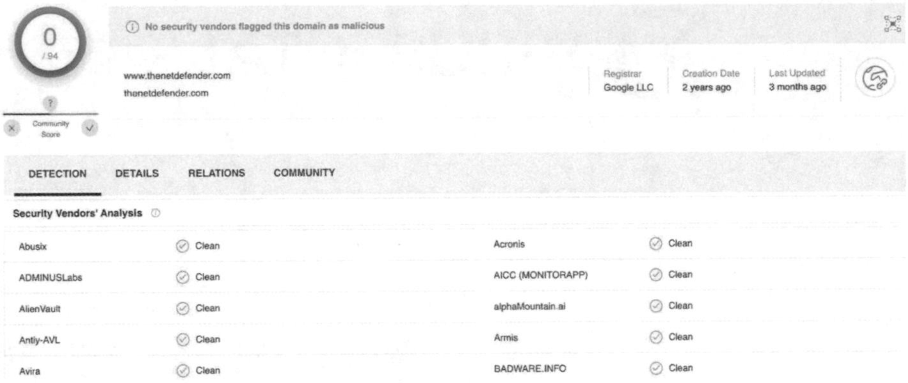


***Figure 5-9.*** *VirusTotal benign link*

Figure 5-10 demonstrates what a malicious page might look like. This link was pulled from an email and submitted for analysis similarly. Thirteen of 87 organizations had classified this as malicious or suspicious. Many of the vendors have classified the suspicious link as phishing or malware in nature. Typically, one or more organizations classifying the link as malicious is a sign that this site should be avoided. VirusTotal, nor any tool, is accurate 100% of the time and should not be used as a sole indicator of the validity of a message. You need to analyze all aspects of the message and make the best-unbiased determination based on your findings.

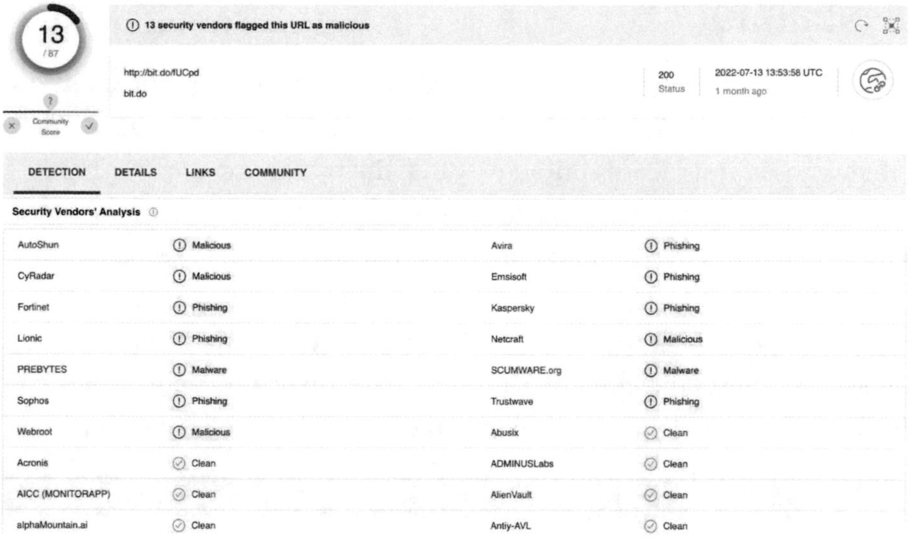


***Figure 5-10.*** *VirusTotal malicious link*

VirusTotal is one of the best tools for link analysis. It provides a safe way to leverage the knowledge and expertise of the world's best and brightest security companies. Sometimes using VirusTotal is not enough, and if a link is new and has never been seen by one of the security companies, it might not have been evaluated yet. The site also could be highly targeted and specifically created for a user. For this and other reasons, seeing the page or resource the sender is trying to point you to might be useful. Visiting the page yourself could be dangerous, but having a service visit the page on your behalf and take a screenshot would be much better. This might sound difficult and expensive, but this is free and takes mere seconds.

# urlscan.io

urlscan.io (`https://urlscan.io`) is a free service that scans and analyzes submitted links. It has an automated process that browses the page like a regular user and records the activity that the navigation creates. The page analysis is stunning, providing a very in-depth analysis leveraging IP information, geolocation services, a screenshot of the page, statistics, and if it classifies the site as malicious. If you can only use one tool for your analysis, urlscan.io is the Swiss Army knife you want in your arsenal. Figure 5-11 shows the landing page for where you begin. Again, safely copy the link of choice, right-click to paste, and select the Public Scan button.

***Figure 5-11.** urlscan.io landing page*

Once the scan is submitted, the page load momentarily while the automated process visits the page. You are then delivered a complete report of the page detailing the information available. Study this information from top to bottom and review the screenshot. You can click the screenshot to view the page but be cautious. Clicking other links on this page could direct you to the site you intended to scan. urlscan.io does not stop you from visiting a malicious site. It only provides a snapshot at a specific time.

For this purpose, however, you want to focus on the screenshot section and the urlscan.io verdict. Refer to Figure 5-12 for more details on the benign page. These are two critical pieces of information that help us determine more about the submitted link. The screenshot is a snapshot of the page. This visually displays what the page looks like in a safe environment. The urlscan.io verdict is the determination made by urlscan.io on the site's validity. Much like VirusTotal, urlscan.io checks security vendor organizations for known signs of malicious activity associated with a site. The completed report has far more information which can be useful as you get more advanced in your analysis, including the IP address, hosting provider, and certificates. For our purposes, let's focus on viewing the page screenshot safely and checking the site verdict.

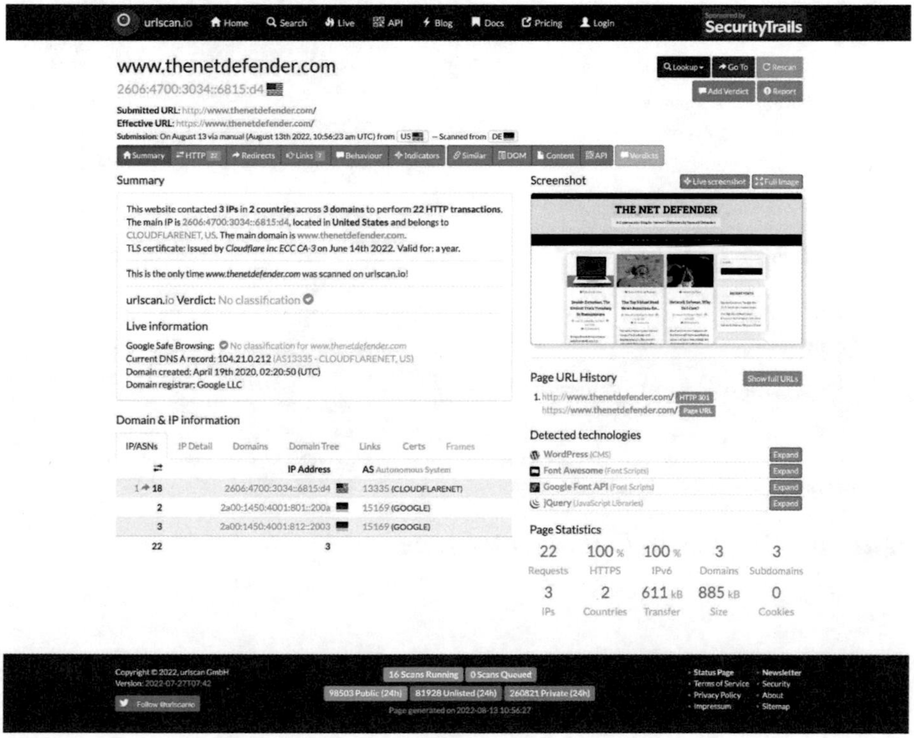


*__Figure 5-12.__ urlscan.io benign page*

Not all sites submitted are benign. For this reason, I have provided a malicious site for reference. Let's submit the link in the same manner as previously explained and again review the screenshot and urlscan.io verdicts. Figure 5-13 shows the urlscan.io report. Reviewing the same sections as the previous submission, the urlscan.io verdict identifies this site as potentially malicious. The screenshot can be viewed as an additional indicator.

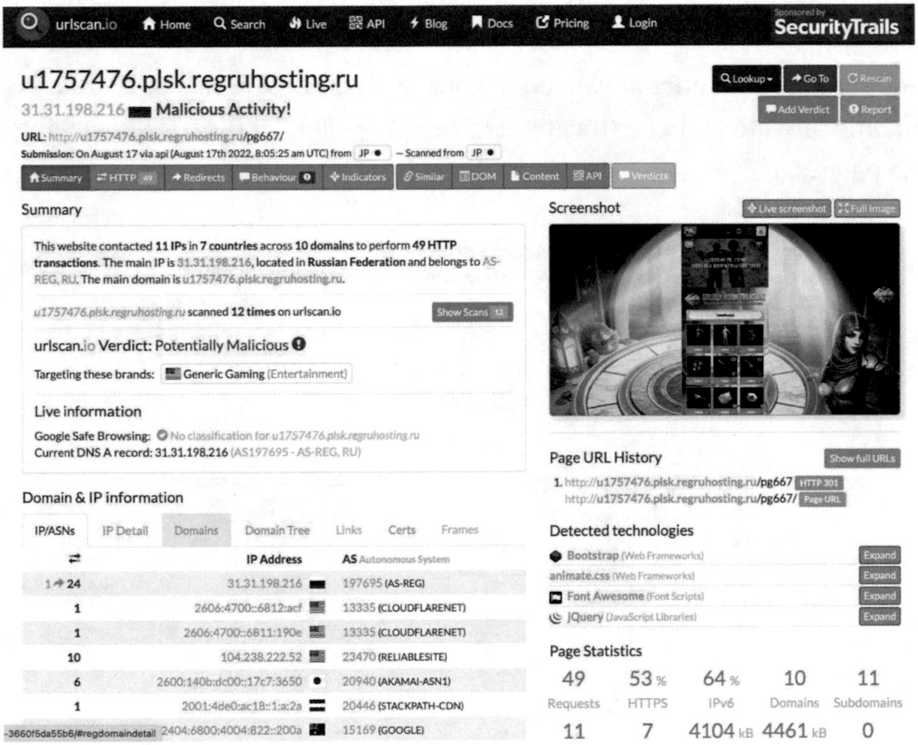


***Figure 5-13.*** *urlscan.io malicious page*

# URLVoid

Sometimes a tool cannot analyze a link or is not functioning properly. For this reason, it is important to always have a secondary or tertiary tool. URLVoid (`www.urlvoid.com`) checks the reputation of a submitted website against a list of security vendors. It is similar to VirusTotal, but they do not share the same security vendors. The process for copying and submitting links remains constant. Figure 5-14 shows the landing page for URLVoid's website reputation checker.

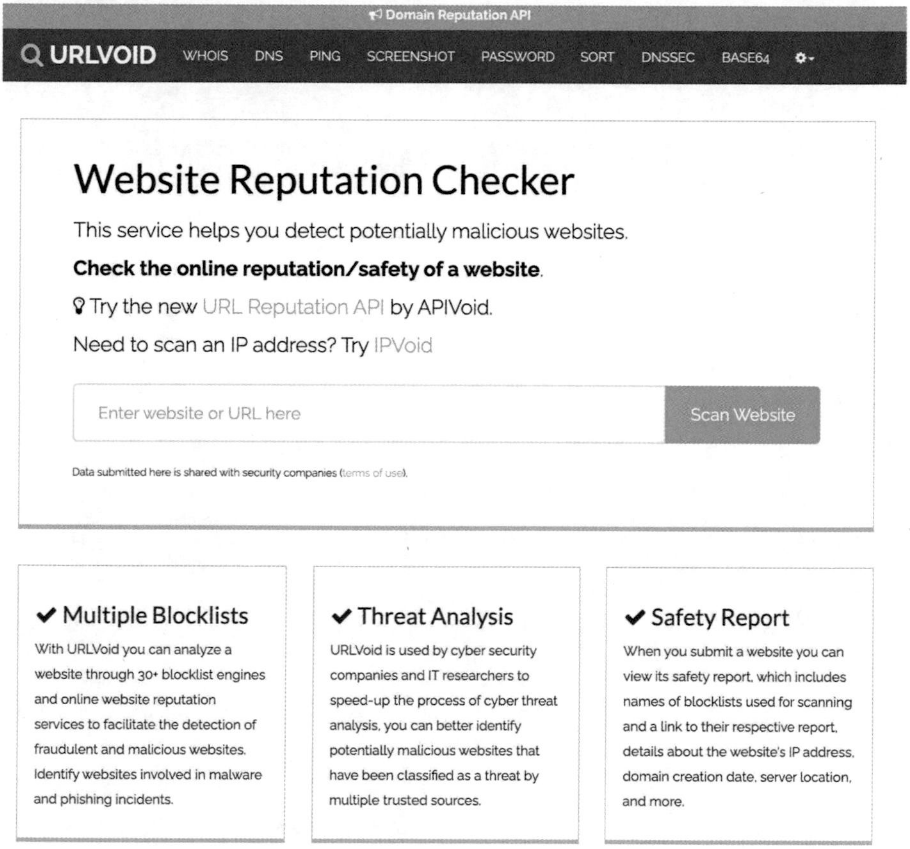


***Figure 5-14.*** *URLVoid website reputation checker*

To submit a link, right-click and paste it in the box and click the Scan Website button. The tool takes a few seconds to run and returns a report on the submitted link. Figure 5-15 shows a site that returned no signs of malicious activity. It is important to reiterate that the results of these tools should not be taken as sole sourcing for the validity of a site. Figure 5-16 shows a site that had signs of malicious activity.

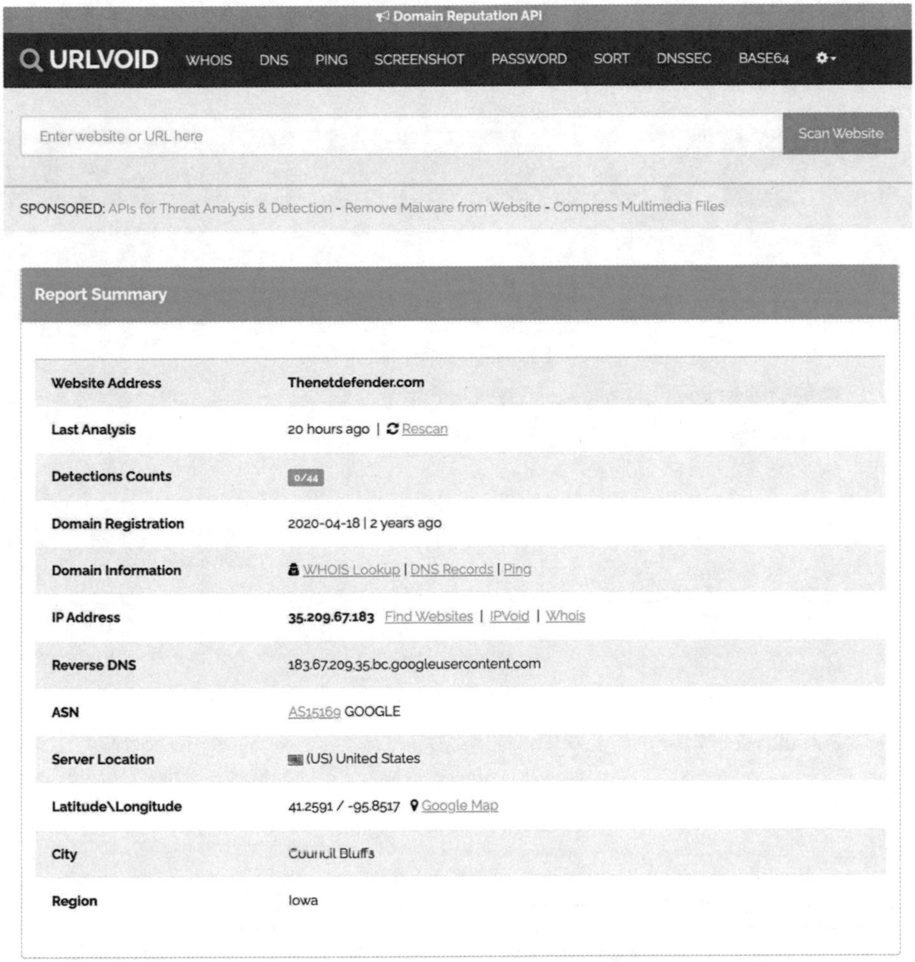


*Figure 5-15.* *URLVoid benign site*

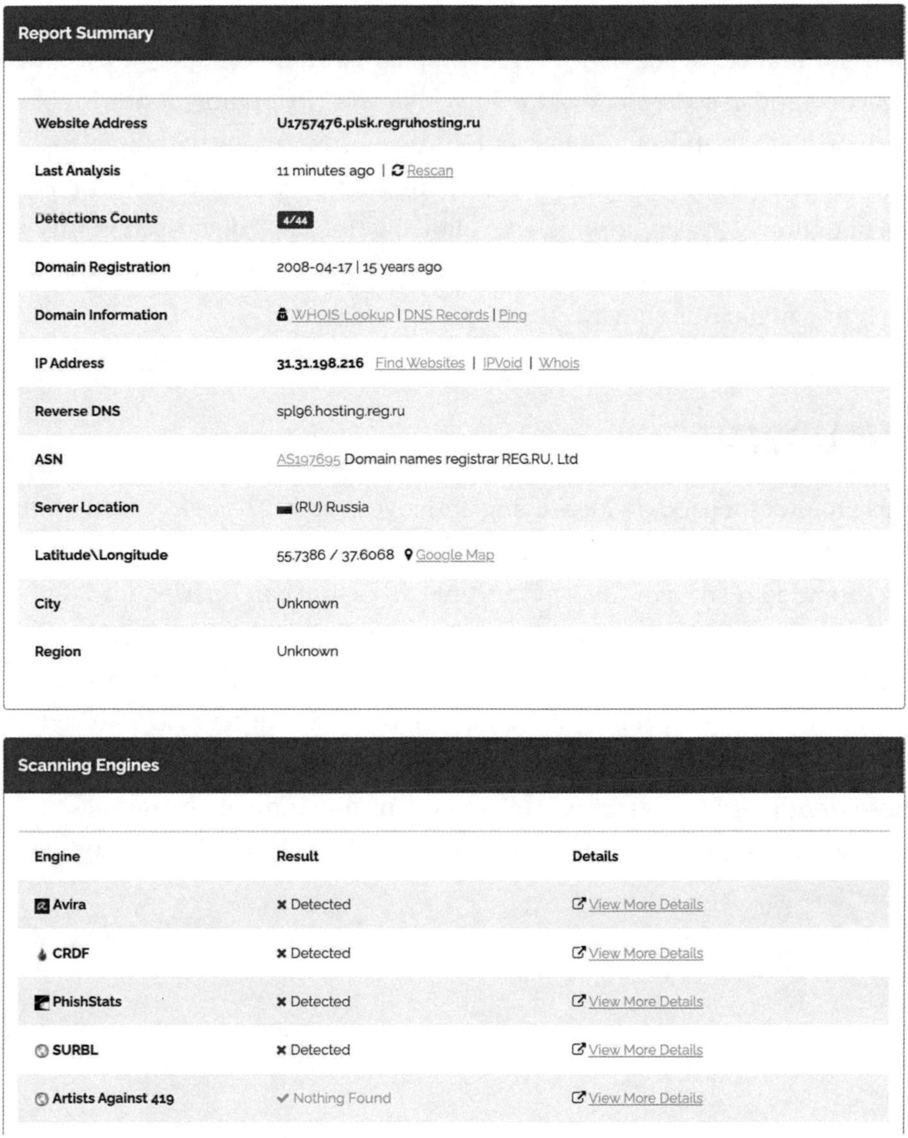


***Figure 5-16.*** *URLVoid malicious site*

You now know how to safely extract links from a website and analyze them for malicious activity. The tools explained in this chapter are highly regarded and used in some of the top cybersecurity organizations in the world. It is important to be cautious when interacting with links in email messages, an error when interacting with an email could result in the machine being compromised. Following the steps discussed in this chapter and exercising caution, give you one more tool in your arsenal for detecting malicious activity.

# Summary

This chapter focused on identifying and investigating links in emails. You learned a safe process to copy links out of emails without interacting with the intended resource. You saw multiple tools that can be used for link analysis to help determine the legitimacy of a link. This is one of the more important chapters because a large percentage of phishing emails use malicious links as a primary infection vector. The chapter also featured some sample content containing links with malicious content; visiting these or other malicious sites can infect your machine. Be extremely cautious when interacting with the malicious links in this book or other materials.

## CHAPTER 6

# How to Handle Attachments

The next component to explore is email attachments. You know now that emails can contain content and links to help convey a message to the recipient. The possibilities do not stop here; attachments can also be included to supplement the links and content. Many attachments are used legitimately, but attackers have taken advantage of this email component and used it to deliver malicious software to recipients.

## What Is an Email Attachment?

An email attachment is simply a computer file sent with an email message. It is attached to the email message and delivered as an additional component of the email message. The file is limited only to the imagination of the sender. This can include an image, video, data, zipped folder, or nearly anything else the sender wants to send digitally. Most attachments sent today are Office documents such as Microsoft Word, PowerPoint, or Excel. The next most common attachment is zipped or compressed files and folders typically containing multiple files. If you've had an email address longer than a day, chances are you've seen or received an email with an attachment. Figure 6-1 lists some common file types that can be used as attachments. This is followed by Figure 6-2 showing an example of an email with a simple attachment.


N. Oles, *How to Catch a Phish*, https://doi.org/10.1007/978-1-4842-9361-4_6

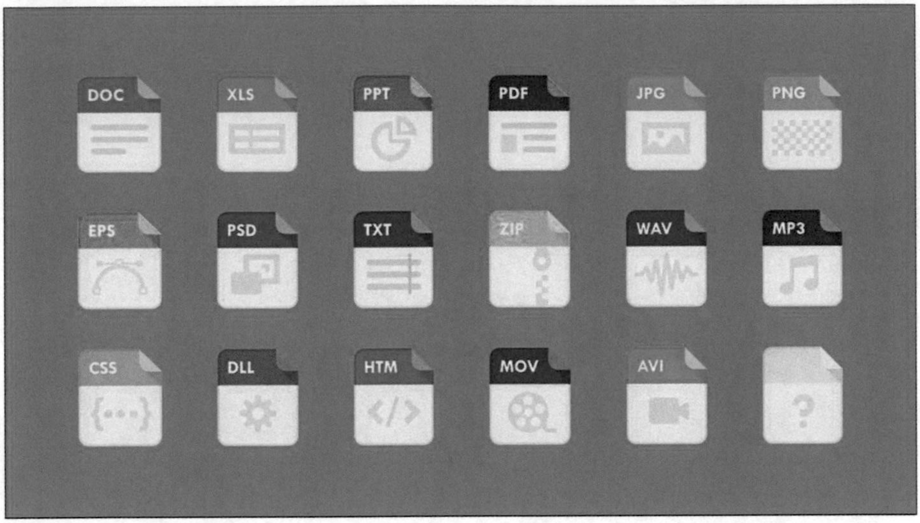


***Figure 6-1.*** *File attachment types*

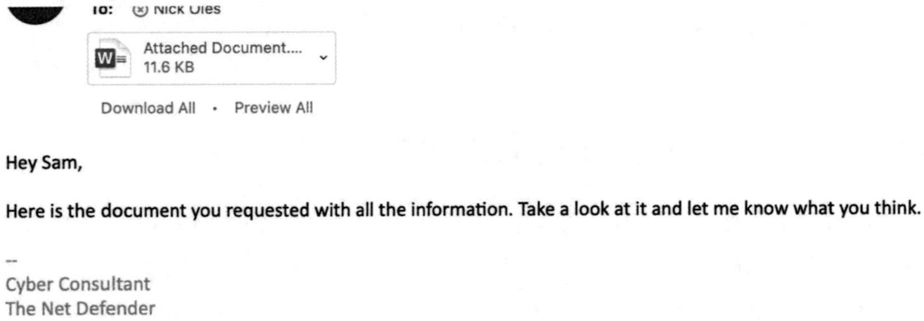


***Figure 6-2.*** *Example email with attachment*

Different mail applications render the email attachment in different formats. Covering how each mail application visually depicts attachments would be extremely time-consuming and not very beneficial. Typically double-clicking the attachment opens the file. If the file contains malicious software or code, it could then execute on your machine similarly to malicious links. What is important to understand is the concept of email attachments. They come in various shapes and sizes and can be used for legitimate and malicious activities. They need to be examined and handled with caution to avoid compromise. Let's discuss some suspicious indicators and tools used to evaluate attachments.

## Does the Attachment Make Sense?

The first and easiest thing to do when evaluating an email attachment is to ask one simple question. Does this email attachment seem normal? The answer may not be a simple yes or no.

Here are some additional questions and explanations to help determine normalcy.

- Would the sender of the email include this type of attachment?

  If you know the sender, would they use this type of attachment? For instance, if someone is responsible for sending you a budget spreadsheet every month that is a Microsoft Excel file, suddenly sends you a Microsoft PowerPoint attachment stating it is the new budget spreadsheet. Would a PowerPoint presentation make sense when expecting a budget spreadsheet that is typically an Excel file? Probably not, and it would be a cause for concern. Make sure that the file type aligns with what the sender claims to be sharing with you as an attachment.

- Did I ask for this document or file?

  This simple question is fairly self-explanatory. Did you request the file that has been sent to you? If not, this might signal someone trying to get you to interact with the attachment. If you requested the file, it is part of your job duties, and the file type makes sense. It is plausible that the attachment is intended for you and is safe. If not, you should think twice before interacting with the attachment since it could be malicious.

- Do I need this information for my job?

  An example of this is a person sending what is conveyed as bonus information for the entire company to the marketing team in an organization. Would the marketing team need to see what every employee received as a bonus for the year? Typically the answer would be no, and the reason it is being sent is malicious. If the attachment isn't meant for you, it probably really isn't meant for you to be opening.

- Does the attachment align with the email content?

  Would it be normal for someone to email you requesting that you view an attachment that is an audio or video file? Use the content as a guide to help you determine what the attachment should likely contain. If this seems off or out of place, it likely is and should be a sign of caution when interacting with the attachment.

These are all questions you want to consider when evaluating the attachment and can also help you with content and link analysis. As you work through the email from top to bottom, ask yourself these questions while looking at all the email components. While doing this, take note of the suspicious indicators and, when complete, review and make the best determination of how to proceed. Sometimes asking these questions won't be enough, and you must evaluate the attachments closer for signs of malicious activity.

# Malware

Attachments come in various shapes and sizes. You can use the content and behavior of the sender to determine some level of confidence in the validity of a message, but in some cases, you need to take this a step further. Luckily, there are tools that examine attachments and provide a report with additional context and information. First, let's discuss a few terms and concepts.

You must first understand the basic concept of computer code before exploring signatures. Computer code is the written language used to execute specific functions on a computer. A human programmer writes the code the computer reads and executes to complete a specific task. This compiled code is often called an application or, more commonly known, a program. Programs provide functionality on a computer and are part of every interaction with a computer.

Malicious software, also known as malware, is written in computer code. The code is used to damage data or software. Malware comes in a variety of shapes, sizes, and levels of complexity. In addition to stealing or damaging data, most malware is written for financial gain of the attackers. In most cases, attackers are trying to monetize the implications of the malware and generate money. This can come in direct payment, sensitive information that can be sold, or access to the infected machine for another party. The intricacies of malware can be a very technical and difficult topic. This book focuses on malware being bad software sent from an attacker to a victim. It is sent to users for bad things to happen, and it is our job to try and identify this and avoid interaction.

# Evaluating Attachments

You now know that attachments contain files capable of many different things and can be safe or malicious. But what if you review the content and behavior of the email and are still unsure? How can you evaluate an attachment if it is potentially dangerous? Luckily, another suite of free online tools allow you to learn more about attachments. The tools discussed operate in two main fashions when evaluating the file for suspicious or malicious activity indicators: static and dynamic analysis.

# Static and Dynamic Reviews

The first file attachment review approach is to scan the attachment statically. It is static because the file is not executed; you are reviewing the code contained in the file. This method determines if the reviewed code matches any known malicious code that has already been previously analyzed and recorded. This known and evaluated code is called a signature. The signature allows us to alert or detect software that a company has deemed malicious. It is important to note that the file is not executed during static analysis. Instead, the code is scanned and checked against known repositories of computer code for matches. Security companies do this thousands of times a day and continuously update a list of ever-growing signatures. As new malware is created, security companies quickly try to create additional signatures to detect and help protect their customers.

The second file attachment review approach is to scan an attachment dynamically. This approach requires us to execute the file in a safe environment and monitor its activity. You can then document what the file does and determine suspicious or malicious indicators. This typically includes closely monitoring the file activity, any website requests, and any new or altered files created. Dynamically analyzing a file is great for new malware not previously categorized. It can help determine the validity of a file based on its actions rather than the code. This approach sounds more difficult than static analysis, but some tools can help.

## Extracting Attachments

Before evaluating the files, let's discuss how to safely collect the email attachments for analysis. This must be a direct and deliberate process to ensure that you handle the attachment in a safe matter and avoid unnecessary risk or potential infection. These files may be malicious, and it is important to act with caution until deemed otherwise. Fortunately, you only need a mouse and a few clicks to start. Our goal is to save the attachment to our computer and not open or execute the file inadvertently in the process.

The first step depends on your mail application. Figure 6-3 shows a menu option on the far right of the attachment; it looks like a downward-pointing arrow. Right-clicking the arrow offers additional features, which include the Save As option. You want to save this attachment, without running it, to use for further analysis. This can be accomplished in many ways, depending on the preferred mail application. I provide a few examples, but these are not the only platforms or ways to save email attachments, but rather a guide to aid in the process you take with your specific mail platform. Figure 6-4 shows a symbol highlighted showing a Download button. Clicking this button downloads the file to a specific location without executing it.

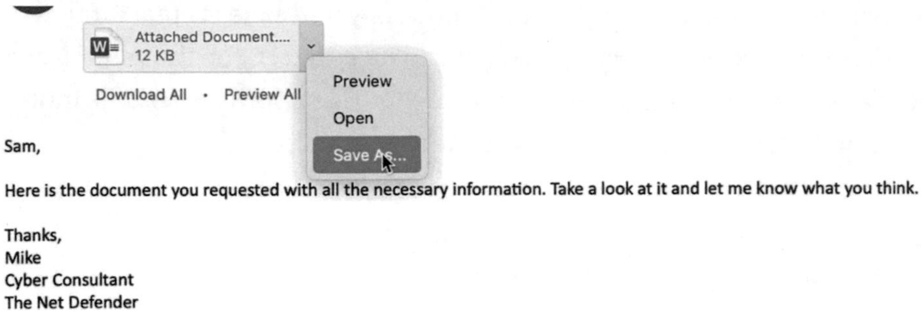


***Figure 6-3.*** *Attachment extraction example*

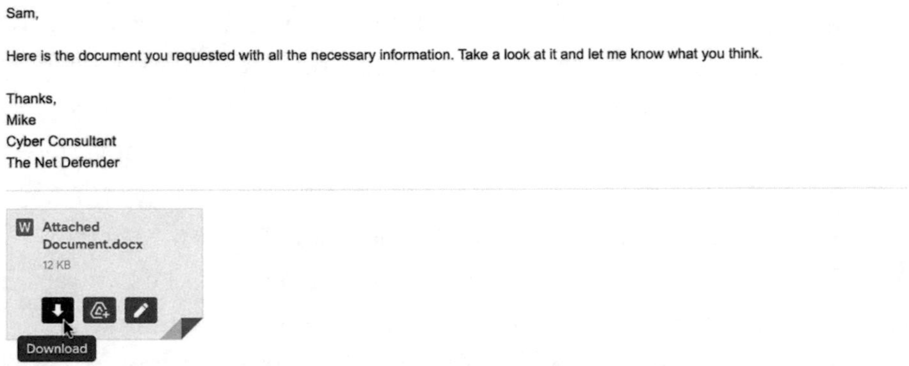


***Figure 6-4.*** *Attachment extraction example*

Once the file has been saved or downloaded, it typically stores the file in the Downloads folder of your operating system unless otherwise specified. You can find this by navigating to this folder on your C Drive in Windows or through the Finder feature on your Macbook.

# VirusTotal

VirusTotal (`www.virustotal.com`) checks a repository of security vendors to identify malicious activity for websites. It also does this for attachments and works in a similar process. In addition to links, VirusTotal conducts static analysis of submitted files. As mentioned earlier, this means the file's code is scanned and checked against a repository of known signatures for malicious activity. VirusTotal then produces a report of the findings, which can aid in determining the validity of the file.

Once the file is saved, visit the same initial VirusTotal webpage to submit the attachment for analysis. Click the File button at the top left of the page, then navigate to the centrally located Choose File button. Once you click this button, you need to navigate to the location of our stored file. In most cases, this is in the Downloads folder on your computer. Figure 6-5 shows the initial landing page highlighting the Choose file button for submission.

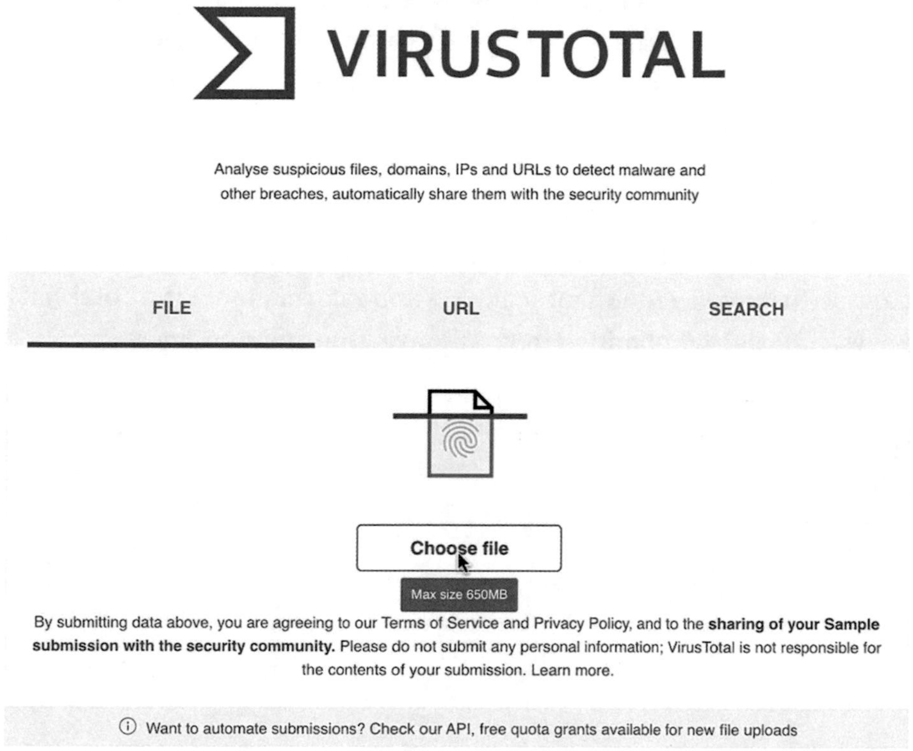


***Figure 6-5.*** *VirusTotal file submission page*

Once the file has been chosen, you can submit it for analysis. The tool quickly produces a hash of the file, which is a fingerprint or unique value assigned to this specific file. Any changes to the file would produce a different hash. The concept of hashing gets more prevalent with advanced analysis. For us, it's just good information to know at our level. VirusTotal takes a few seconds to analyze the file and check against its repository. If no known security vendors have identified this file as malicious, you will receive a report like the one shown in Figure 6-6.

The file submitted in Figure 6-6 shows that 0 out of 62 vendors classified this file as malicious. You can tell this by looking at the top left of the page. In the center of the page are additional details of the file analysis process, including the size, name, and when the file was last scanned. VirusTotal checks internally to see if a submitted file has previously been scanned. If the file has been scanned previously, it produces the most recent report. If not, it runs a new report for the submitted file. In large phishing campaigns, it is common for hundreds or thousands of users to get the same link or attachment. This could result in the same attachment or link being submitted multiple times to a tool such as VirusTotal for analysis. To remove redundant scanning and information, VirusTotal can review a previously submitted report to save time and resources.

***Figure 6-6.*** *File submitted with no malicious flags*

Figure 6-7 shows a file submitted with multiple malicious flags. This time in the top left, 9 out of 60 security vendors identified the file as malicious. Looking again at the file details in the center of the page, this is a .zip file and was submitted on August 29. VirusTotal has provided us with a hash for the file and listed the nine security vendors that have identified this file as malicious. Next to each security vendor is the detection name for the signature that identified this file. The signature name can sometimes allude to additional details about what the file does. Figure 6-6 shows BitDefender on the second column of security vendors. Next to BitDefender is the signature as JS.Heur.Backdoor.2.9930B40D.Gen. This likely means the file submitted is malicious and used as a backdoor for actors to enter the system. You ascertain this information from the signature name that lists Backdoor with unique numbers and characters.

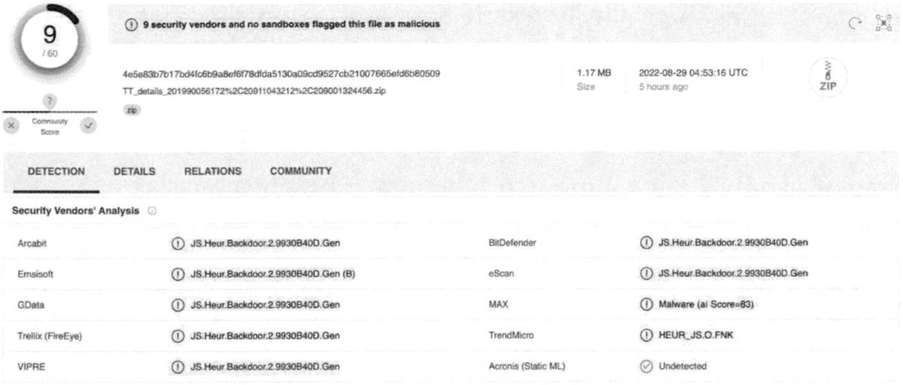


***Figure 6-7.*** *File submitted with malicious flags*

VirusTotal was used to statically scan a file and tell us more about the file in question. Specifically, what if any security vendor has classified this file as malicious? If any security vendors have flagged the submitted file, you should proceed very cautiously because it is likely malicious. You can learn more about the potential nature of the file by looking at the name of the signature provided by the security vendor. If the file returns no flags, that does not inherently determine that the file is safe to interact with. It is possible that no vendors have seen the file previously, or this is a new attack for which signatures are not yet available. For this reason, it might be necessary to use additional tools to execute the file in a safe environment.

## Sandboxing

You previously discussed static and dynamic analysis. You know that dynamic analysis is when the file is executed in a safe environment and monitored for suspicious activity or changes to the system. A sandbox is a specially prepared environment that mimics an end-user personal computer or device. The sandbox prevents compromise by blocking communication out to the Internet, containing no user or critical data, and maintaining the ability to restore and remove any previous artifacts. Sandboxing can be done in hardware, software, and web or cloud-based environments. Utilizing a web or cloud-based service is the easiest and most reliable method to run a file in a sandbox. Let's explore a cloud-based dynamic sandbox environment to aid our attachment analysis.

## ANY.RUN

`www.any.run`

ANY.RUN is a free online tool offering both web-based sandboxing and link analysis. Access to ANY.RUN requires a user to sign up for the platform using a valid email address. It is available to anyone with an Internet connection and can quickly execute a file in a controlled environment for analysis. Once a file is submitted, it creates a detailed report of any suspicious findings. When registered and logged in, you begin this journey at the home page shown in Figure 6-8. To submit a file for analysis, click the New Task button in the top left of the screen.

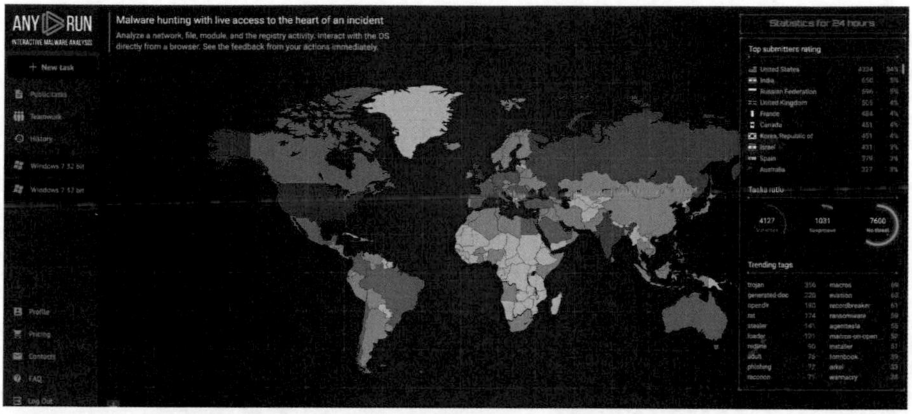


***Figure 6-8.*** *ANY.RUN landing page*

When clicking the new task, a dialog box shows the new options. Figure 6-9 shows the available options for the new task. Here you have the option to submit a file or URL. To analyze an attachment, select the Upload button on the right side of the box and navigate to our saved attachment. Next, select the desired operating system. This is the virtual system the file is executed on. Once this is done, select the Run a Public Task button.

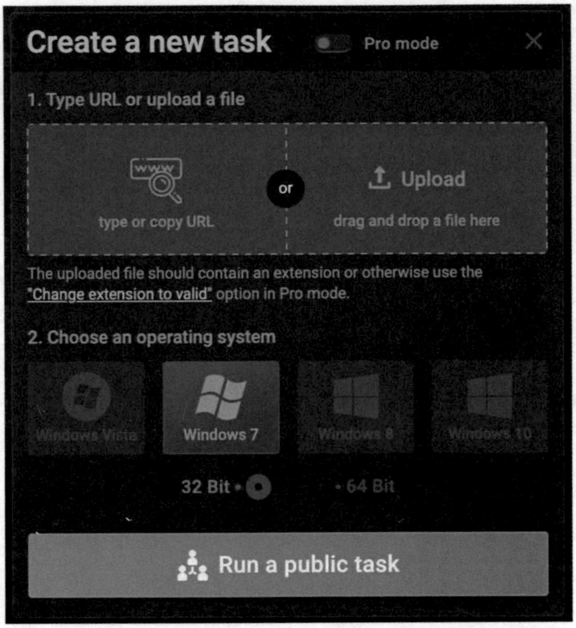


***Figure 6-9.*** *Create a new task dialog box*

Before proceeding, you must acknowledge that the submitted file is available to the public and not be kept private. This should not be a problem in most cases unless you are in an advanced cybersecurity organization. Figure 6-10 shows the "Public task" acknowledgment box; select I Agree to proceed.

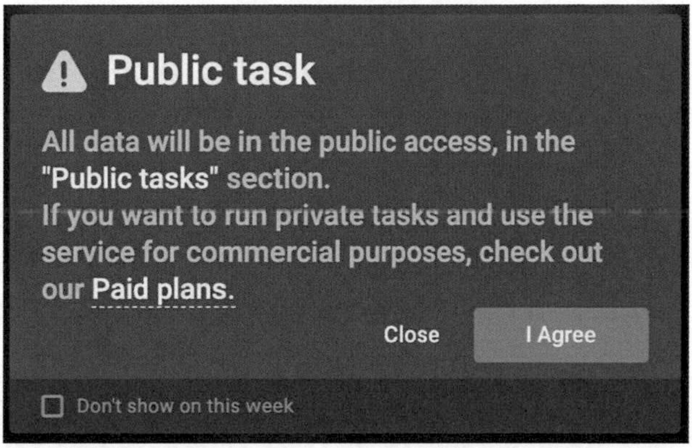


***Figure 6-10.*** *Public task acknowledgment*

Once submitted, it takes a few minutes for the file to process. Upon completion, you are directed to a page similar to Figure 6-11. As you examine this page, you start with the left side of the screen, which shows a screen capture of the file executed in our virtual operating system. This sample file contained a simple Word document with no malicious activity. The screen capture shows the document opened and a preview of what is contained in the file.

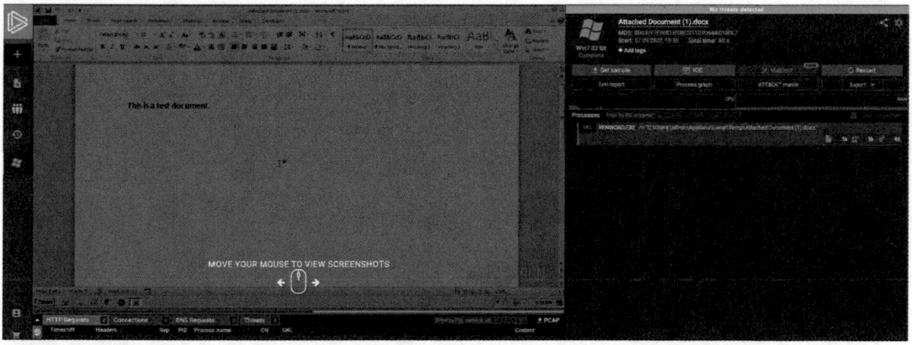


***Figure 6-11.*** *ANY.RUN benign file submission*

On the right-hand side are the file details. At the top is the file name, which for this example is Attached Document (1).docx. You then see the file hash, start time, and total time run. There are a series of additional buttons and a list of all the executed processes in Figure 6-12. The first box allows you to download the sample file. Since you submitted the file, this is not very useful to us but could be for security researchers. The next option is labeled IOC, which stands for *indicator of compromise* and contains specific details or clues that can identify compromise associated with this particular file. The MalConf is not available in the free account, and the Restart button restarts the machine and runs the sample again.

Moving to the second row reveals more report and graphics-based options. The Text Report button leads us to a detailed technical description of the file submitted. The process graph shows any processes executed by running this file. A *process* is a set of instructions executed to complete a task. Executed files often call processes to complete tasks. This behavior and the specific processes can be signs of malicious activity when analyzed. Finally, there is the ATT&CK matrix. The ATT&CK matrix is a set of techniques attackers use to accomplish a specific objective. The details are outside this book's scope, but you can learn more at attack.mitre.org.

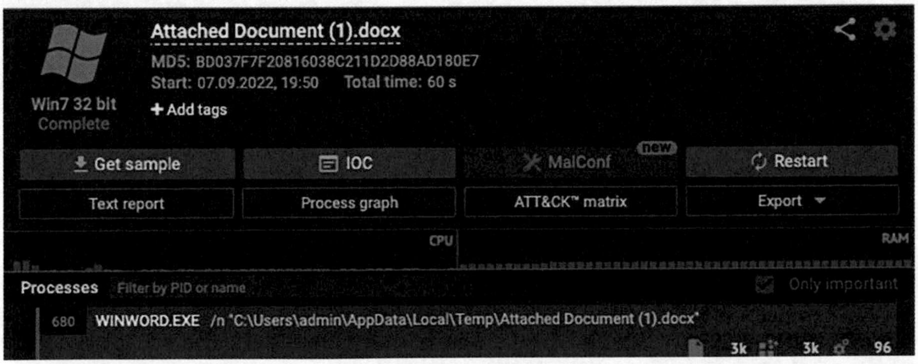


***Figure 6-12.*** *ANY.RUN file report details*

Figure 6-13 shows a sample malicious document. The left pane shows that an application has been executed and a password box has appeared. The right side of the page shows that ANY.RUN has flagged this file as malicious. The file has several processes that are executed that have been identified as malicious. You can learn more by exploring the various details and reports made available.

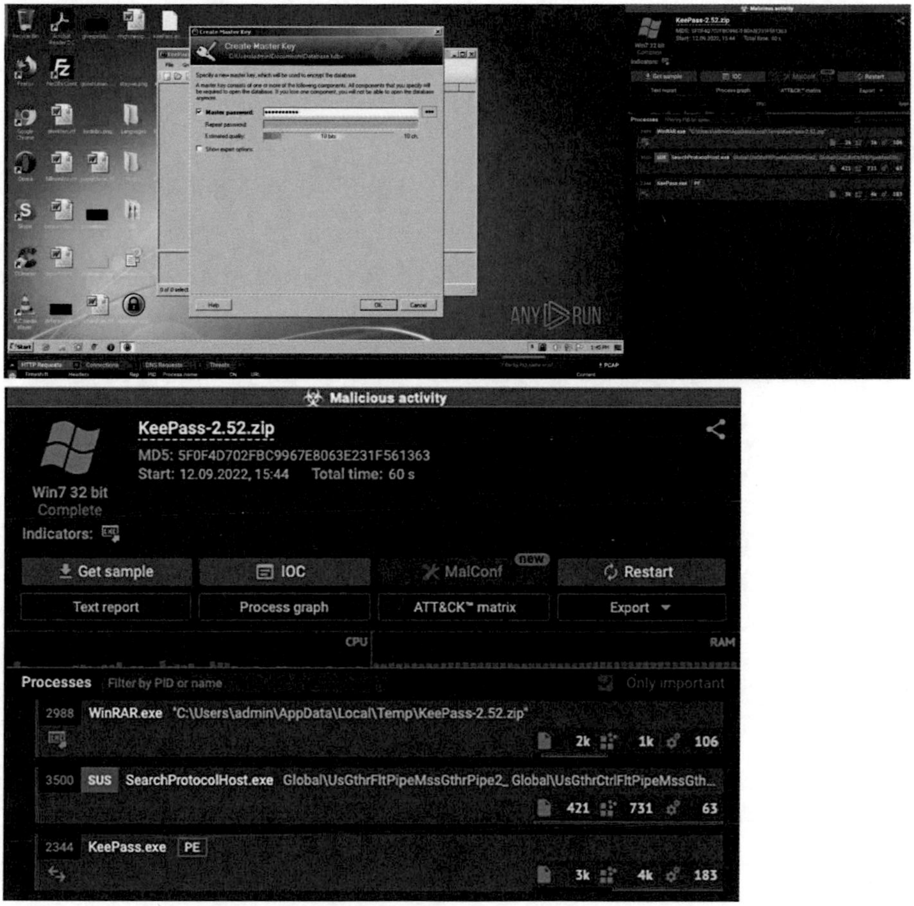


***Figure 6-13.*** *ANY.RUN malicious file*

The report from 6-13 has flagged this file as suspicious and identified processes that indicate malicious activity. This is a strong indicator of a malicious file, and it would be highly recommended not to execute this on your personal devices. Other tools exist for dynamic file analysis, and it is advantageous to have additional options for analysis. Hybrid Analysis is another great option for dynamic analysis.

## Hybrid Analysis

`www.hybrid-analysis.com`

Hybris Analysis is a web-based sandboxing and link analysis tool. Much like our previous tool exploration, you must safely save the attachment for submission and navigate to the Hybrid Analysis home page. Figure 6-14 shows the home page for file submission. Centrally located on the page is the file submission button with the instructions Drag & Drop For Instant Analysis. You can drag the saved file to this box or click for the file explorer to appear and locate the file in question for analysis.

***Figure 6-14.** Hybrid Analysis file submission*

Once a file is selected, an additional box appears to help prepare the environment for your file submission. This has been captured in Figure 6-15, where you see the file name you selected. For our example, we chose the file named Attached Document (1).docx. The first box under the file name allows you to provide an email address for notification when the analysis has been completed. This will email you when the file is completed and provide a link to the report. This is unnecessary for most files as the analysis typically completes rather quickly, but it can be a good feature to take advantage of. Below the email box is a comment section where you can provide additional context for your records. This might include the email sender, identifying context, or the topic of the message to allow you to reference this at a later date and time if needed.

Below the comments section, there are a few options and a captcha. Options include three boxes, with only one being mandatory to proceed. To proceed, you must consent to the Terms & Conditions and Data Protection Policy to submit a file for analysis. You should review these terms closely, but the files submitted are shared amongst the community. This typically only becomes a concern for specific malware or advanced cybersecurity organizations. For most users sharing the sample is not a major concern. The remaining boxes can be checked based on your preferences to share the information submitted. Finally, you have a captcha that determines that a human submitted the request and not a computer-automated process. Check the captcha box at the bottom and select continue.

***Figure 6-15.*** *Hybrid Analysis file submission details*

Once you select Continue, you are brought to a pop-up box displaying the options available for the analysis environment. This is the operating system that the file is executed on. Ideally, you select the same operating system you are using to mirror how the file would act on your PC. Unfortunately, that isn't always possible. For our example, let's select Windows 7 32-bit and click the Generate Public Report button, as seen in Figure 6-16.

***Figure 6-16.*** *Hybrid Analysis environment details*

Once the file is processed, it displays a report of its findings. The report is captured in Figure 6-17 with a summary of the analyzed file. At the very top are the file details, which show us the file name, size, type, and hash. If any threats are identified, they are shown both on the top right of the screen and within the Anti-Virus Results section. Our antivirus results are provided by three reputable security vendors: CrowdStrike, MetaDefender, and VirusTotal. The report summary is at the top of the page, and more detailed technical information is below. Not all files submitted are clean. Figure 6-18 shows a malicious file report you can examine more thoroughly.

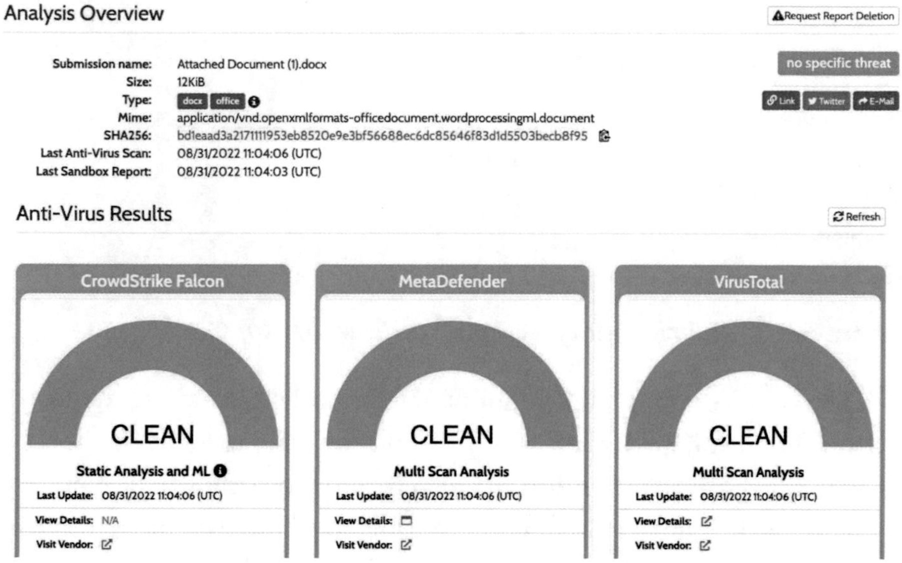


***Figure 6-17.*** *Hybrid Analysis Report With No Indicators*

The file submitted in Figure 6-18 has multiple suspicious and potentially malicious indicators. The top right of the report shows that the file is classified as malicious with a threat score of 100/100. This information is useful, but you should look closely at the technical details to see why this file has been classified as malicious.

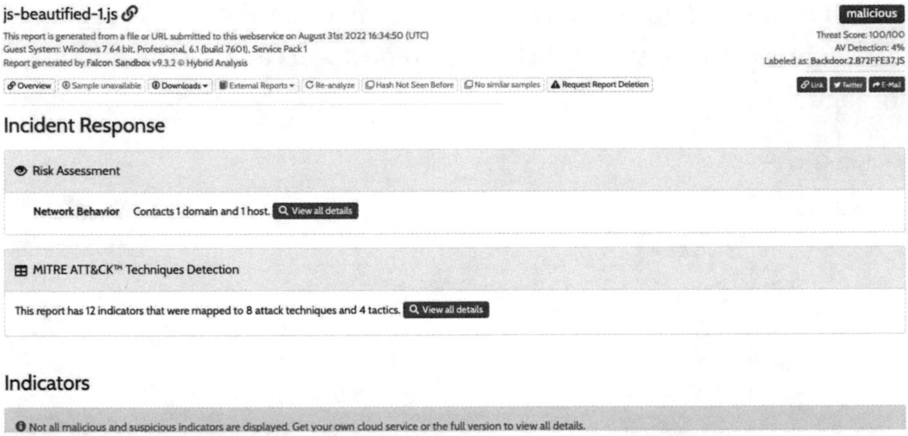


***Figure 6-18.*** *Hybrid Analysis report with indicators*

The report contains a vast amount of technical information, much of which is outside the scope of our process. You want to focus on the malicious and suspicious indicators to help add more information in determining the file's legitimacy. For this file, there are two indicators, as shown in Figure 6-19. The first indicator is network-related and has an IP address and port number the file tried to contact.

Suspicious network traffic is typically a sign of malicious activity, as most files do not need to interact with an external website. This is often seen as a sign of malicious software checking into a controller, delivering additional instructions. The key here is that if a file communicates with an external IP address that is not expected, it is a sign of potential malicious activity.

Unusual Characteristics is the name of the next set of indicators. The details here show that a script, or sequence of computer instructions, produces Internet activity and is obfuscated. This aligns with the previous malicious indicator and is not regularly seen in email attachments.

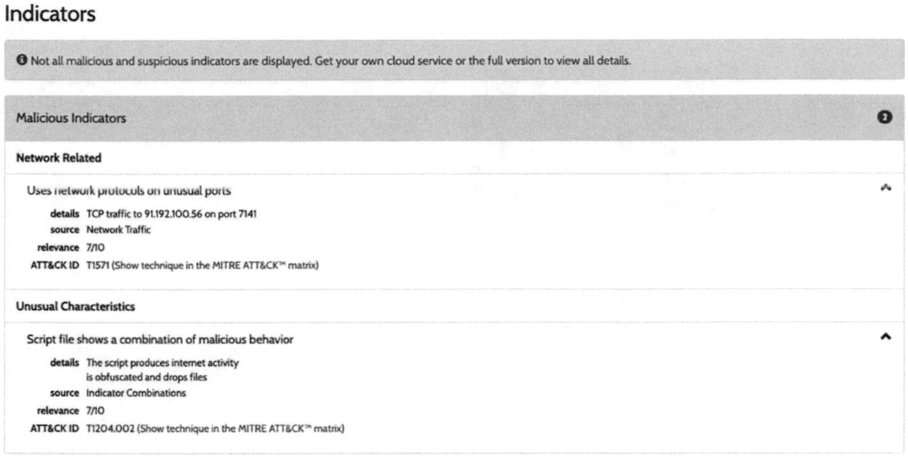


***Figure 6-19.*** *Malicious indicators found*

After reviewing the malicious indicators section, seeing a visual snapshot of any activity that occurred when the file was executed could be useful. The screenshot feature captures an image of the desktop once the file is executed. If a pop-up box, web browser, or another application is launched, it may show here in the screenshot. Reviewing this and determining if this is expected activity can be another indicator of malicious activity. In addition to the screenshot, the Hybrid Analysis section shows any analyzed processes. These processes were deemed suspicious. The chart lists the process details. Figure 6-20 shows a screenshot and the Hybrid Analysis section of the report. The screenshot identifies no activity for this file, but a suspicious process is identified.

***Figure 6-20.** File screenshot and Hybrid Analysis*

The final section to review is the Network Analysis section. Network activity can be a strong indicator of malicious activity in a file. If you think logically, for example, would it make sense for a Microsoft Word document to communicate with an IP address in Switzerland? Does my business have any customers or activity in Switzerland? Chances are that most Office files are static documents containing information that is being shared between two parties. You should consider this when evaluating a specific file type and its associated activity. Very rarely does it make sense for abnormal network activity to occur, and it is something you can only see when executing the file.

The Network Analysis section of the report shows detailed information on the traffic generated from the file. This can be seen in Figure 6-21, which shows the DNS requests, contacted hosts, and contacted countries. The tool reveals that the IP address and domain are in Switzerland. In most cases, this would not be expected, but it takes some analysis from the recipient to determine what is a normal activity.

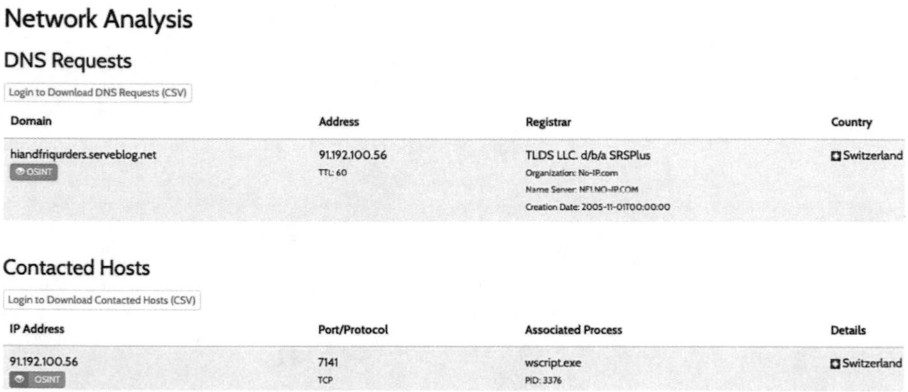


***Figure 6-21.*** *Network Analysis report findings*

# Summary

This chapter reviewed the basics of email attachments and ways to identify suspicious attachments. You learned the fundamentals of static (think code review) and dynamic (think file execution) analysis and explained how some tools could aid your analysis. The tools explored in this section can scan attachments and gather signs of potentially malicious activity before interacting with them on your computers. Attachments can be used in both malicious and nefarious ways; understanding how to identify signs of suspicious attachments and tools to evaluate attachments are critical to catching a phish.

CHAPTER 7

# Log Searching and Response

This chapter explores log records on a local machine and from a centralized repository. This section is useful to home techies, security analysts, and technicians working in corporate environments that might ingest and store log sources from multiple devices for correlation. Now might be a good time to start if you work in a corporate environment and aren't storing log records. Tell your boss you have a great idea that pays huge dividends when an incident occurs. First, let's discuss local logs that are stored natively on Windows devices and then discuss searching using common log repository tools.

## What Are Logs?

A log is a time-stamped record of a particular event occurring on a computer. The record is of an activity that often involves an application on the computer. These log sources help explain activities that occur on a computer and can correlate activity with specific times.

Although Linux logs are also prevalent, this book focuses on the Windows operating system and Window log sources. Log records are rapidly generated every few seconds detailing what occurs on a Windows


N. Oles, *How to Catch a Phish*, https://doi.org/10.1007/978-1-4842-9361-4_7

machine. They are stored locally on the machine and viewable in the Windows Event Viewer. This easy-to-use program lets you review and search for log records on your local machine. The Windows Event Viewer is installed natively on all modern versions of Windows.

So, the Event Viewer can show you the logs, but how do you get to it? You can find it by searching for Event Viewer using the magnifying glass on your taskbar or following these instructions: **Start menu ➤ Control Panel ➤ Administrative Tools ➤ Event Viewer**.

The Event Viewer (see Figure 7-1) organizes your local log sources and allows for quick and easy access for viewing. It is important to note that the log sources stored in the Event Viewer are not natively saved externally to the program and, thus, typically, are overwritten within a few hours. It is often referred to as "logs rolling", which means newer log records overwrite older log records as they come in. If anyone mentions that the log records have likely rolled, they are no longer available.

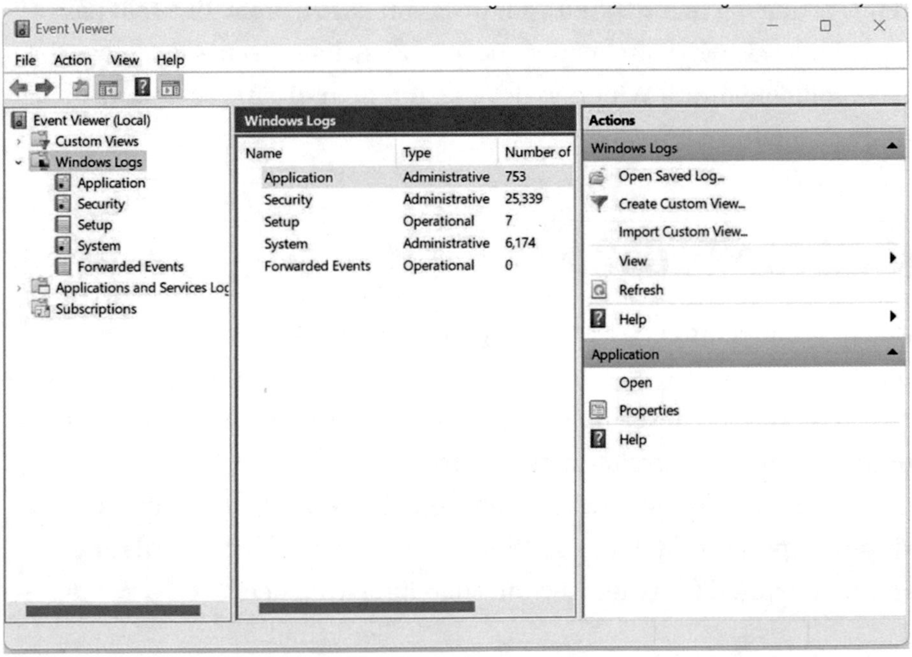


***Figure 7-1.*** *Windows Event Viewer*

Select the Windows Logs on the far-left panel in the Event Viewer. Expanding this menu option reveals five subfolders. The following are brief descriptions of each.

- **Application**: These events are related to a software or application hosted on the computer, such as the starting, stopping, installation, or errors occurring with a specific program being executed or run on the computer.
- **Security**: These events are triggered by the systems audit policy and are used to track events such as login and logout information, failed login attempts, and other security-related activity.
- **Setup**: These log records contain information for all actions that occur while the operating system or applications are installed.
- **System**: These are events are driven by system components such as drivers. Drivers are installed to allow the operating system and a device to communicate.
- **Forwarded Events**: It allows events to be sent from one host to another. The events can then be stored on a separate host and saved for review at a later date and time. This helps eliminate the log rolling issue and can play major dividends in incident response activities and investigations.

Next, let's look at the different types of log records. Windows has the following five different log types.

- **Information**: Typically means the application or service is operating normally. These are low-level alerts or records typically showing normal activity. A large volume of these are generated throughout normal operations.
- **Warning**: These hint toward potential issues that may occur. The log records show signs of a potential issue or problem that may occur if no further action is taken. An example might be warning messages for low or unavailable storage on a device.
- **Error**: These events are more serious and are usually associated with a system malfunction. Software crashing or failing to open might have error log records that provide more detail. Error messages are probably the most useful when troubleshooting issues or suspicious activity on a machine.
- **Success Audit**: This log type shows valid authentication attempts to a computer or network with the correct credentials. It happens when you log into your laptop or desktop using the correct username and password.
- **Failure Audit**: These are the opposite of the success audit logs. They show failure to access or authenticate to a computer or network. It occurs when the incorrect username or password is used to access a resource.

The various categories and types of log sources can help explain what the log record shows in the system. Reviewing log records is a good troubleshooting approach to learning more about a technical problem on a pc and determining the next appropriate action. Figure 7-2 shows an example log record for a successful logon event.

If you accidentally clicked on a suspicious link or attachment when examining an email, reviewing the local log records on your PC might provide additional context into what happened and where to look next. Pay special attention to the Security, Application, and System logs. Since these logs are generated rapidly, try and search as close to the time you received and interacted with the email as possible. The log records contain details about the logged event, which include the event ID, level, date and time, and the task category. These details can help further investigate any suspicious activity from the email.

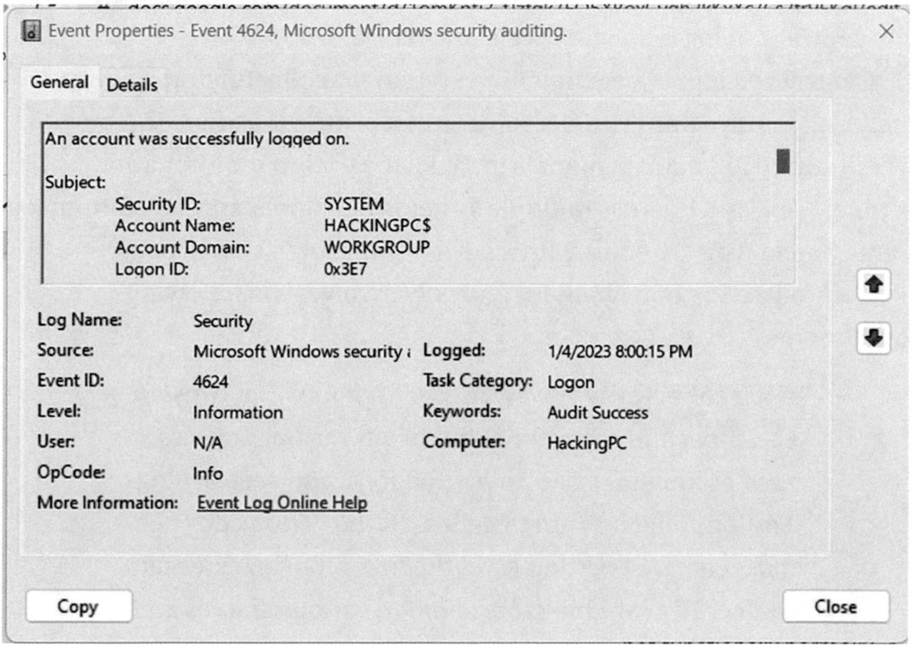


***Figure 7-2.*** *Windows event log example*

## Centralized Log Management

All computer and networking devices generate log records. The busier the device, the more log records it generates. A router or switch with multiple connected devices constantly sends data and generates thousands of logs in minutes. These logs are quickly rolled or overwritten if not shipped off somewhere for storage. Centralized log management sends multiple log sources from multiple devices to a specified location for storage. As you can imagine, the number of logs grows rapidly, and it is soon very difficult, if not impossible, to use and search through these log records, which is why centralized log management is important.

Centralized log management is a system for collecting, storing, and analyzing log files from various sources in a central location. The purpose of centralized log management is to make it easier to monitor and troubleshoot issues across multiple systems and applications. Without log management, you are stuck with a large volume of useless data.

Centralized log management typically involves the following components.

- A **log collector** is a software agent or tool that runs on each host and collects log files from various sources, such as system logs, application logs, and security logs. The log collectors are installed on the various devices that generate logs and send the logs off to an external source. The log collectors come in various shapes and sizes and are versatile.
- A **log aggregator** is a central server or service that receives log data from the log collectors and stores it in a centralized repository, such as a database or a file system. Typically, this is a server located on the network that can communicate with the various

devices generating logs. The log collectors select and forward the relevant log records to the aggregator for storage.

- A **log analyzer** is a tool that allows you to search, filter, and analyze the log data stored in the centralized repository. It enables you to identify patterns, trends, and anomalies in the log data and generate reports and alerts. For security analysts, this is the most important piece of the puzzle. The analyzer lets you filter and investigate log records searching for the relevant desired information. Log analyzers are among the first places for most incidents when starting an investigation.
- A **log viewer** is a user interface that allows you to view and interact with the log data stored in the centralized repository. It provides a view into the actual log records that can be used for further investigation or evidence.

Centralized log management helps improve the systems' security, availability, and performance. It also enables IT teams to troubleshoot problems, identify and respond to security threats, and comply with regulatory requirements. You've heard about how great and useful log management can be, but what tools can you use?

# Security Onion and Splunk

Chances are, if you work in an environment that conducts log management, you use a paid or free service. The top two platforms for log management from a cybersecurity perspective are Security Onion and Splunk. Security Onion is a free platform allowing users to collect, sort, and search log records. The only cost for the business or user is the hardware needed for the software to run on. Splunk is the industry-leading log management tool for cybersecurity customers and is typically paid on a subscription model. Other tools exist, but discussing every tool available today would be nearly impossible. Let's focus on the two most popular platforms.

## Security Onion

Security Onion is a Linux distribution designed for network security monitoring (NSM) and event correlation. It is based on Ubuntu and includes several open source tools for network analysis, such as Snort (an intrusion detection system), Suricata (another IDS), and Sguil (a security information and event management tool).

Security Onion also includes many other tools for network analysis, such as Bro (a network analysis framework), ELSA (an event-based logging and analysis system), and OSSEC (a host-based intrusion detection system).

One of the key features of Security Onion is its ability to automatically detect and analyze network traffic to identify suspicious activity. This is done through intrusion detection and prevention systems known as Snort and Suricata, which can detect a wide range of network-based attacks. These systems use pre-defined or custom-made rules to detect and alert on identified traffic that may be malicious or suspicious.

Another important feature of Security Onion is its ability to collect and store large amounts of network data for analysis. It is done using Sguil, designed to help security analysts quickly and easily search through large amounts of network data. Sguil is useful for analysts searching for phishing email records to see how many people at the organization were targeted, when the emails were sent, and any unique characters that can be identified from the metadata.

In addition to its core features, Security Onion has other NSM and analysis tools. For example, it includes tools for visualizing network data, such as Kibana and Grafana, and tools for automating network data analysis, such as Moloch and Squert.

Overall, Security Onion is a powerful and flexible NSM and analysis tool. Its combination of open source tools and automation capabilities make it well-suited for use in a wide range of security-related tasks, from incident response to threat hunting.

You can download Security Onion for free from securityonionsolutions.com. Locate the Software tab to take you to the webpage to download the software (see Figure 7-3).

***Figure 7-3.*** *Security Onion download page*

Setting up Security Onion is not instructed in this book. Several online tutorials and resources have been created to assist with this. The Security Onion website also offers instructions for installation and setup.

## Splunk

Splunk is a mostly paid software platform that allows users to collect, analyze, and visualize machine-generated data from a wide variety of sources. Splunk does offer a free version for small amounts of data, but most organizations quickly outlive this restriction and need a paid model. Splunk is commonly used for log analysis, security, IT operations, and business intelligence.

One of the key features of Splunk is its ability to collect data from various sources, including log files, network traffic, and system metrics. This data can then be indexed and searched using Splunk's powerful search engine, allowing users to quickly and easily find the information they seek. Figure 7-4 is a sample image of the search engine used for Splunk.

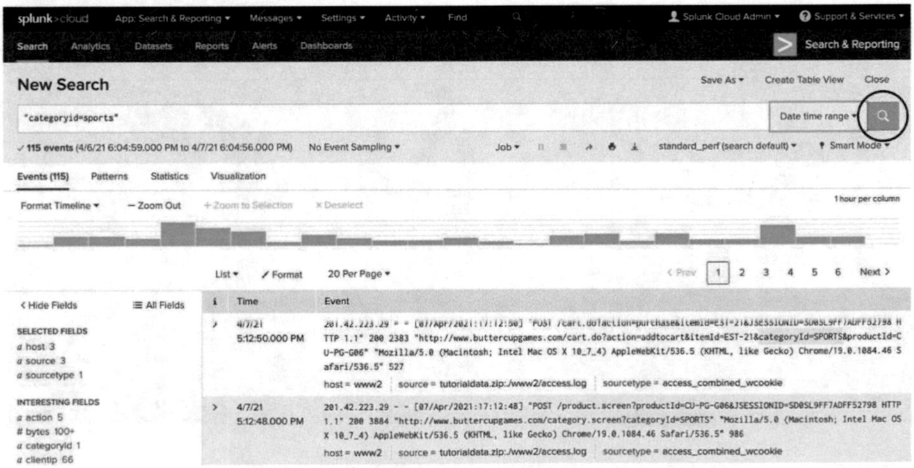


***Figure 7-4.*** *Splunk search engine*

Another key feature of Splunk is its ability to analyze and visualize data in various ways, such as using pre-built dashboards and reports and creating custom visualizations using Splunk's built-in visualization tools. Analysts love this feature as it helps explain complex technical findings in simple charts and graphs. Figure 7-5 shows an example of a dashboard created in Splunk.

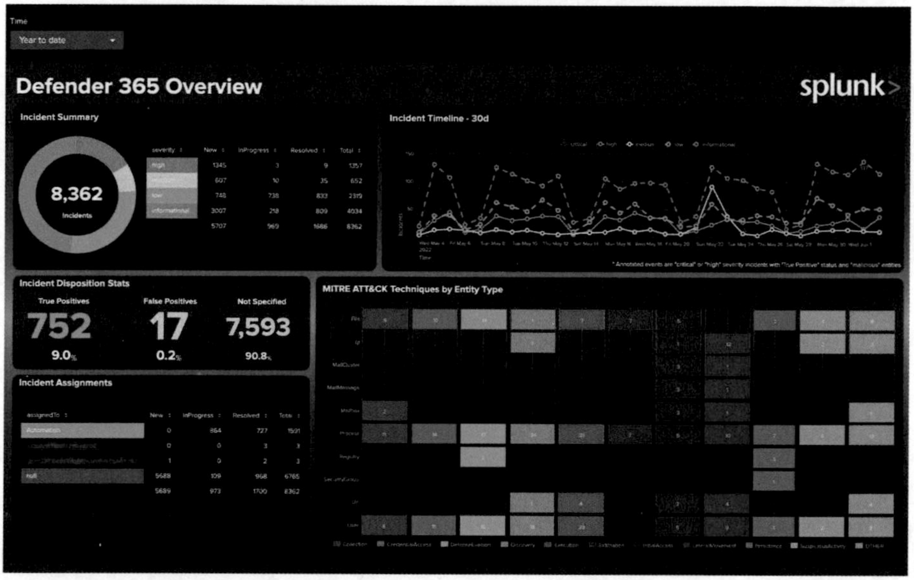


***Figure 7-5.*** *Splunk dashboard*

In addition to its core features, Splunk includes several other tools and capabilities that can aid in data analysis and visualization; for example, tools for real-time data analysis, machine learning, predictive analytics, and a software development kit that allows users to create custom applications and integrations.

One of the most powerful aspects of Splunk is the ability to create and use search commands that allow users to retrieve specific information from the indexed data and perform specific actions such as filtering, counting, sorting, and transforming the data. This allows an analyst to strategically filter and review results as needed. Figure 7-6 shows some search commands applied to sample data.

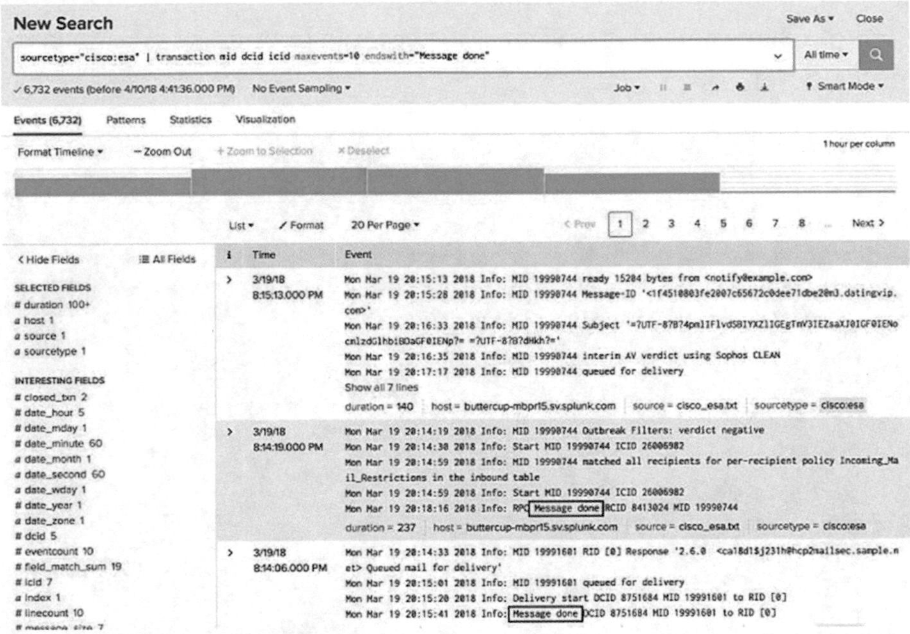


*Figure 7-6. Splunk search commands*

Overall, Splunk is a powerful and flexible software platform well-suited for use in a wide range of data analysis and visualization tasks. Its ability to collect and analyze data from many sources and powerful search and visualization capabilities make it a popular choice for organizations of all sizes. Splunk offers many free courses to learn about the product offerings and how to use them. Training is at Splunk.com; navigate to the Free Training tab shown in Figure 7-7.

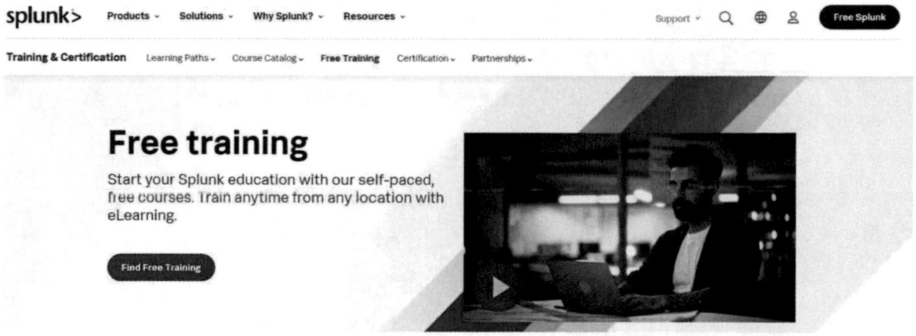


***Figure 7-7.** Splunk offers free training.*

Both Splunk and Security Onion store and categorize data differently depending on the data provided and the specific configurations. If you can ingest email log records, you should be able to search through logs and find metadata records, such as date/time, subject, sender, recipient, IP information, and email size. When a phishing email is reported or investigated, these centralized log management tools can help you quickly identify how widespread the issue may be. With simple search terms, you can determine how many emails were sent, to whom, and when they were delivered. I recommend the following search approach to identify the targeted audience of the attacker.

1. Search for the sender's address. This tells you if the specific sender sent emails to other individuals in the organization.

   If a unique sender address, try and use the domain if possible. It might be something like *@thehacker.com. Depending on the domain, it could be easy or difficult.

2. Search on the subject of the reported email. It might be something like Invoice #444353. The subject might be specific to the campaign or randomly generated for each recipient.

3. Search the specific time the email in question was sent. Chances are the emails came in around the same time and could lead to additional context in the investigation.

4. Combine some of the criteria when possible. It might include using the domain of the sender *@thehacker.com and searching for a specific time range. It could lead you to find additional email addresses the attacker was using.

   You could also try the size of the email or the sender's IP. Both of these can get tricky depending on the configuration of your mail environment.

This chapter covered some fascinating stuff regarding log records in this section. If it seems like a lot of information at once, it might make sense to revisit this a few times. Log records on computers are critical for incident response as they provide valuable information about the activity on a system. This information can be used to detect and diagnose security incidents, track down the source of a problem, and determine the extent of the damage.

# Summary

This chapter explored log records and how valuable they can be when investigating incidents. Log records can be reviewed on any computer and aid in troubleshooting benign and nefarious activities. You learned how to search these records and some of the information that can be contained in various records. Go ahead and try it out. Review some log records on your own devices!

# CHAPTER 8

# Remediation and Lessons Learned

Thus far, this book has largely discussed identifying and detecting phishing messages and suspicious activity deriving from email messages impacting a computer or network. Once you identify this behavior, what should you do next? You learned the PICERL process and are nearing the final stages of our incident response process. These stages include eradication, remediation, and lessons learned. When complete, this closes out our process and brings our systems back to a normal state while analyzing what you've learned.

I discussed and demonstrated how to detect and handle a suspicious email message, but what should you do with the message once identified? Should you simply delete the message, ignore it, or share it with all of your friends? The answer lies somewhere between these responses and depends on your internal factors and circumstances. In many cases deleting the message makes sense. However, if you want to help improve detection methods and help prevent others from receiving similar email messages, most mail applications allow the ability to report or block a suspicious message.

Reporting suspicious messages allows a security team or automated process to analyze the message, adjust security controls, and help protect others. When a message is reported, it gets broken down in a similar process explained in the book, and key indicators are removed.


N. Oles, *How to Catch a Phish*, https://doi.org/10.1007/978-1-4842-9361-4_8

The indicators include sender, recipient, subject, malicious links, and attachments, all of which are used to detect and block future messages from being delivered. This process is conducted manually or automatically by a series of super smart computer programs and people.

Reporting messages helps improve and secure the mail environment for everyone. This practice helps the security teams identify what they missed and attempt to prevent future messages from being delivered. Reporting is not mandatory, but it is a nice way to use what you've learned and try and help out other security enthusiasts like yourself to get better. Most mail applications have a built-in reporting button or option that quickly forwards and deletes the message from your mailbox. If you work in a corporate environment, the internal security team should have a process for reporting suspicious emails. If they don't suggest this be implemented, it is an easy process to set up and encourages employees to report suspicious activity. Figures 8-1, 8-2, and 8-3 are screenshots of how to report messages in Gmail and Outlook.

In Gmail, click the three vertical buttons at the far right of the message. A list of additional options appears, and you simply need to click the Report Phishing button. The message is then sent to Google's security team and deleted from your mailbox. An additional dialog box appears detailing what happened upon reporting the message.

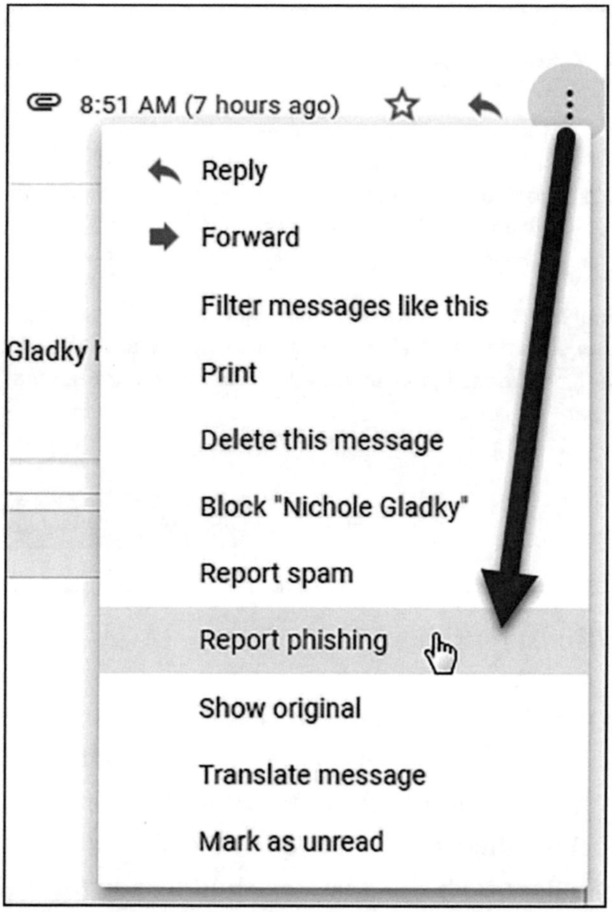


***Figure 8-1.** Report phishing in Gmail application*

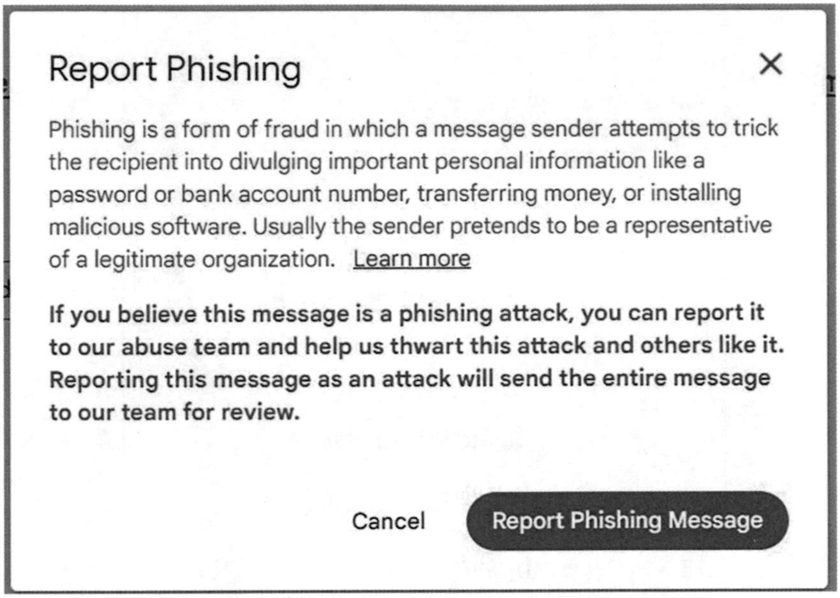


***Figure 8-2.*** *Report phishing notification*

As seen in the phishing notification dialog box, Google describes phishing, and the Learn More button provides additional details and descriptions. The notification informs the user that reporting phishing messages help them thwart this attack and others like it. To finish the process click the Report Phishing Message button, and the message is then removed from your inbox.

Microsoft Outlook handles phishing email reporting a little differently. Natively, Microsoft Outlook only provides the ability to report messages as junk. These are categorized more generally but tend to associate spam and marketing emails and malicious phishing messages. The Junk reporting button is located on the Home ribbon in Outlook, this can be seen in Figure 8-3. By clicking the drop-down button, you can block the sender. The Junk E-mail Options feature provides additional email options to help prevent messages from the specific sender from being delivered.

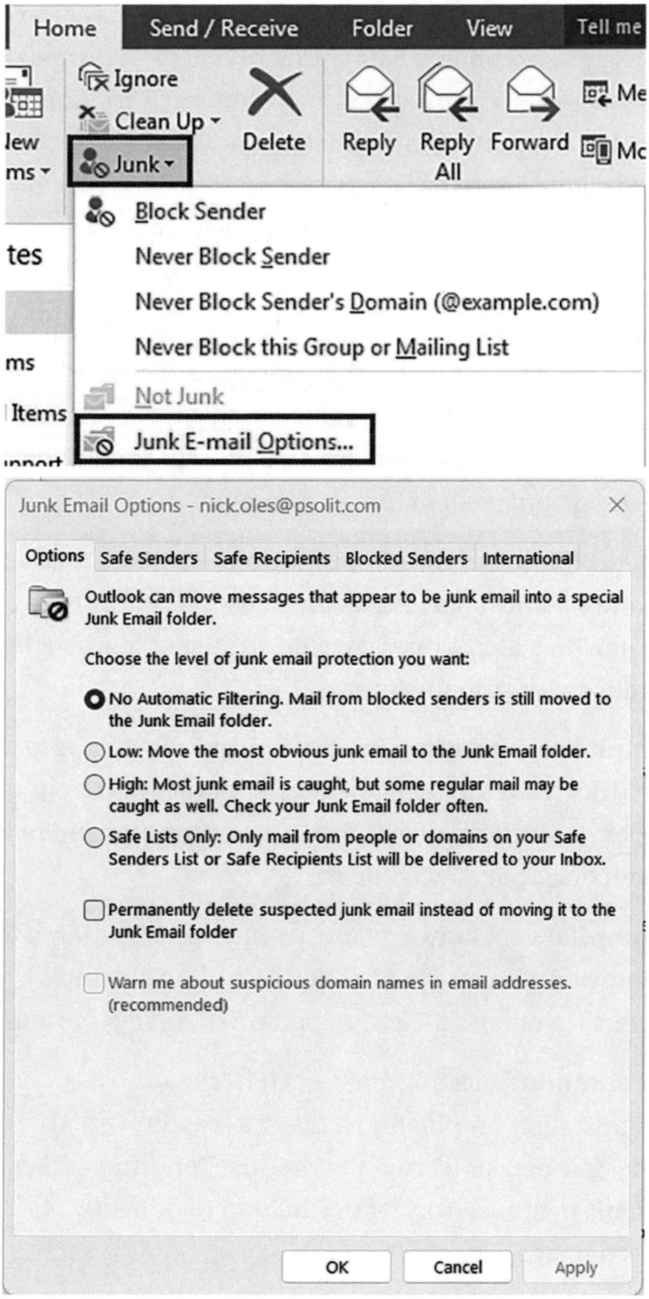


***Figure 8-3.*** *Outlook junk options*

A built-in process does not natively exist to enable users to report phishing messages in Outlook. Rather that needs to be turned on and managed by the Outlook administrators in your organization. If the security team has a reporting mechanism, you should learn and use the process they designed to report messages.

Reporting phishing emails to your security team is important for a few reasons.

- **Early detection**: Phishing emails can be used to gain unauthorized access to an organization's networks and systems. By reporting phishing emails to the security team, the organization can take action to contain the incident and prevent further damage.
- **Identification of trends**: Reporting phishing emails to the security team allows the team to identify trends in phishing attacks and develop strategies to prevent similar attacks in the future.
- **Employee education**: Reporting phishing emails to the security team can help to educate employees about the types of phishing attacks they may encounter and how to recognize and avoid them.
- **Compliance**: Many regulatory requirements mandate reporting of security incidents, including phishing. Failure to report can lead to penalties and legal issues.
- **Reputation**: Phishing emails can harm an organization's reputation if they successfully steal sensitive data or disrupt operations. Reporting phishing emails to the security team can help to mitigate this damage.

This activity is important for protecting an organization's networks and systems, identifying trends in phishing attacks, educating employees, compliance, and protecting the organization's reputation.

Once you have identified that an email is malicious and gleaned all the necessary information, what should you do if you don't want to report the email? Why is the best solution to simply delete the email? The email has no legitimate purpose or uses on our device, and it can only lead to additional potential compromises and issues if left alone. What if you are searching through your email months from now, and you accidentally click an attachment from a malicious email? All that hard work you put in to detect and avoid this phishing email has vanished, and you are back at square one. Deleting an email is very straightforward; I provide some basic instructions that should work with all mail applications.

You can select the email message and hit the Backspace or Delete button on your keyboard, which should delete the message and move it to the Deleted Items or Trash folder in your mailbox. This simple method removes an unwanted email from almost any mail application in the world. Each application also has a delete button on the web or client. application You should be able to quickly identify these buttons, and if not, a simple Google search leads you to the proper ways to delete an email using your application of choice. Figure 8-4 shows the delete button in the Gmail and Outlook mail applications.

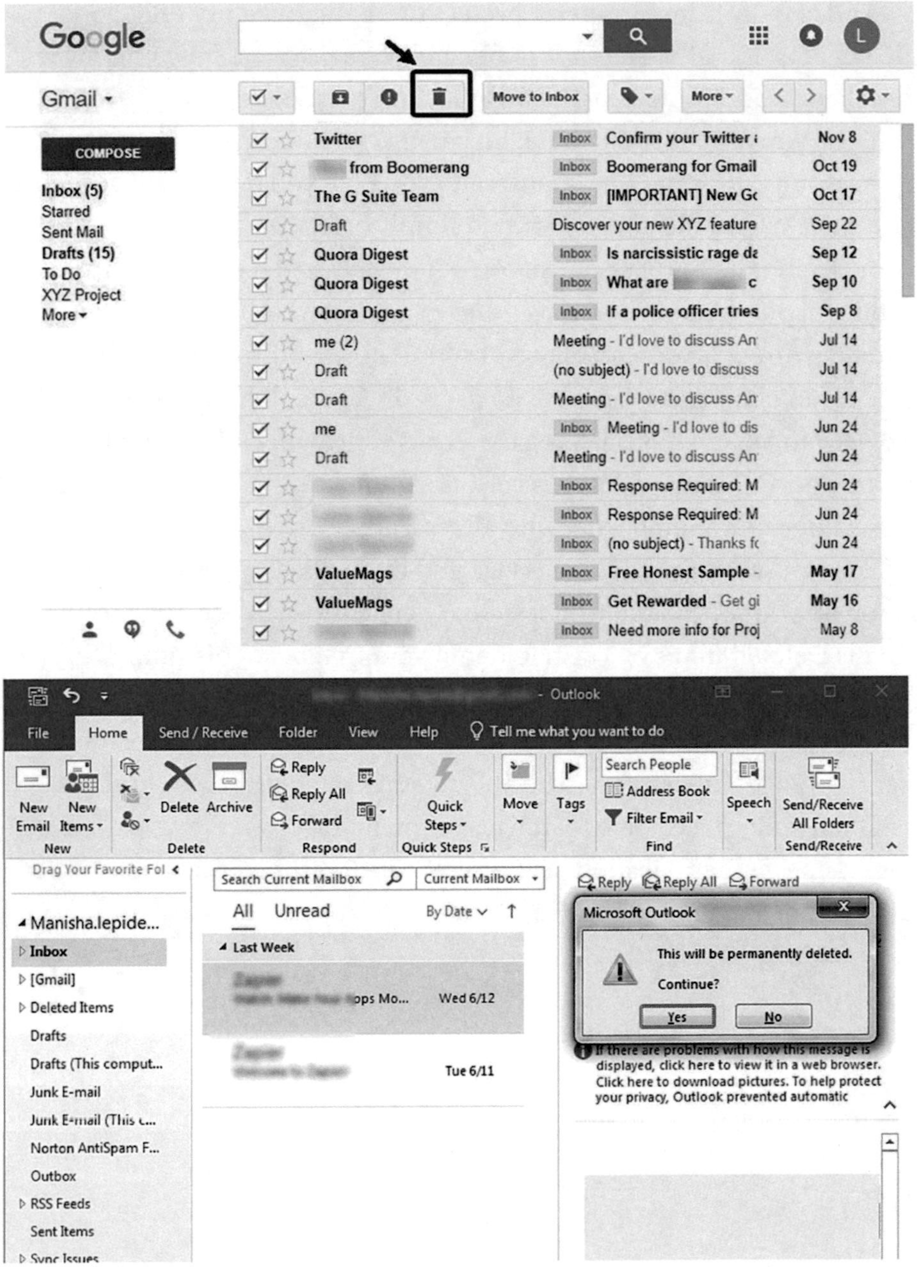


***Figure 8-4.*** *Deleting email messages*

You've learned how to report a message if you want to; if not, you can simply delete the message. But what if you accidentally click one of those pesky links or attachments you are trying to avoid? This could infect your machine with malicious software, commonly known as malware, and may impact your machine's operation or the data stored on your device. If you suspect your machine is impacted by malicious software, remove it quickly. In our process, this is the eradication stage in which you strive to remove unwanted software from your device with as minimal impact as possible.

Eradication involves permanently removing a threat or vulnerability from a system or network. Eradication can be accomplished through a variety of methods.

- **Removing malware**: Malware, such as viruses, worms, and Trojan horses, can be removed from a system using antivirus software or manual methods. This may involve running a full system scan with your native antivirus system, installing and running a program created to remove the malware, or manually deleting infected files.
- **Resetting accounts**: Accounts compromised in an attack may need a reset and new credentials issued. In some cases, if a password is hardcoded or cannot be reset, the account should be deleted, and a new account be created. If you provided your username and password as part of a phishing email, you should immediately reset the password for any impacted accounts or accounts with shared passwords.
- **Employee training**: Employee training can also be considered a method of eradication. By educating employees on how to spot, remove, and avoid phishing, suspicious links, and other attack methods, they can reduce the chance of falling victim to cyberattacks or repeating behavior.

The most common eradication methods are removing malware and resetting accounts. Most phishing emails are sent to install malware or harvest account credentials. In many cases, malware is removed by an antivirus application installed on the device. Windows operating system computers have Windows Defender installed and run natively. If you have a Windows machine that is not running antivirus, stop reading this book and go install antivirus! Microsoft has made major strides in information security, and its antivirus software works great for most home and professional users. However, if you want an antivirus with different features or capabilities, you have many options, usually for around $100 a year or less. The following is a list of common antivirus applications that work great at stopping malware.

- Symantec
- McAfee
- Trend Micro
- Bitdefender
- Avast
- AVG
- ESET
- F-Secure
- Avira
- Sophos

Each antivirus program must be installed, updated, and continuously run to detect and remove malicious software. The great thing is that once installed and configured, this should all happen automatically. Each application has a different interface, but the suggested programs can conduct the following tasks with the proper configuration.

- Update automatically. This involves new detection mechanisms for malicious software. The detection methods are called *signatures* and *triggers* based on identified computer code or behavior. New signatures are released daily and must be updated to provide protection.
- Schedule scans. This prompts the antivirus program to scan the computer's hard drive for malicious files. The scans run in the background and check each saved file against a repository of malicious files for matches. These are typically run daily or weekly. I recommend a daily scan if possible. If files are detected, they are deleted or quarantined. Deletion is better than quarantined.
- Real-time scanning enabled. Many programs offer real-time scanning or a similar feature in which the antivirus software scans live programs while running on the machine. This helps catch applications not installed on the hard drive and stored in memory on the device. The intricacies of programs running in memory versus on disk are outside this book's scope. For our purposes, just know that real-time scanning monitors files as they are executed and run in memory while scheduled scans monitor files saved on the hard drive.

If you find that the antivirus software cannot remove the malware, you may need to install and run another program for removal. One of the best programs that specializes in removing malware is called Malwarebytes. Malwarebytes is an anti-malware software that detects and removes malicious software, including viruses, trojans, worms, spyware, and other potentially unwanted programs from a computer system. It offers real-time protection against online threats and can scan for malware on demand. This is a great supplement to run in tandem with your antivirus software. It can help detect and remove malware your antivirus software fails to detect. An initial trial version can be run for 14 days on your computer, which can help remove a pesky malware file you cannot get off of your pc. If you still want to use the program after the trial period, it costs you a few dollars a month. At the time of writing this book, it was under $5 a month for personal use. See Figure 8-5 for the Malwarebytes homepage.

*Figure 8-5. Malwarebytes webpage*

Downloading the program is a simple task that takes just minutes to get up and running. Selecting **Free download** or **Personal plans** sends you to the install page identified in Figure 8-6. A setup file called MBSetup.exe is downloaded; it must be run on your computer.

***Figure 8-6.*** *Malwarebytes download page*

Click the MBSetup.exe file once downloaded to start the installation process. An installation wizard appears that walks you through the program's installation (see Figure 8-7). The default recommended settings are good for getting Malwarebytes up and running.

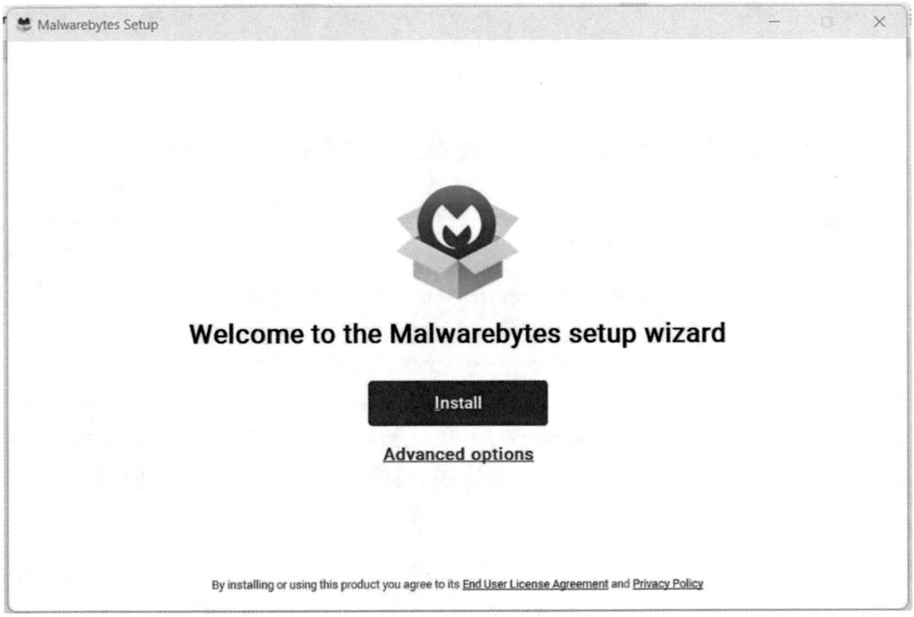


***Figure 8-7.*** *Malwarebytes install wizard*

When the installation is complete, your system may need to be rebooted. Upon reboot, you can launch the program and scan your PC. It can be executed in a few minutes with instant access to your results. Once the application has been started, you simply need to click the Scan button in the lower center of the screen (see Figure 8-8).

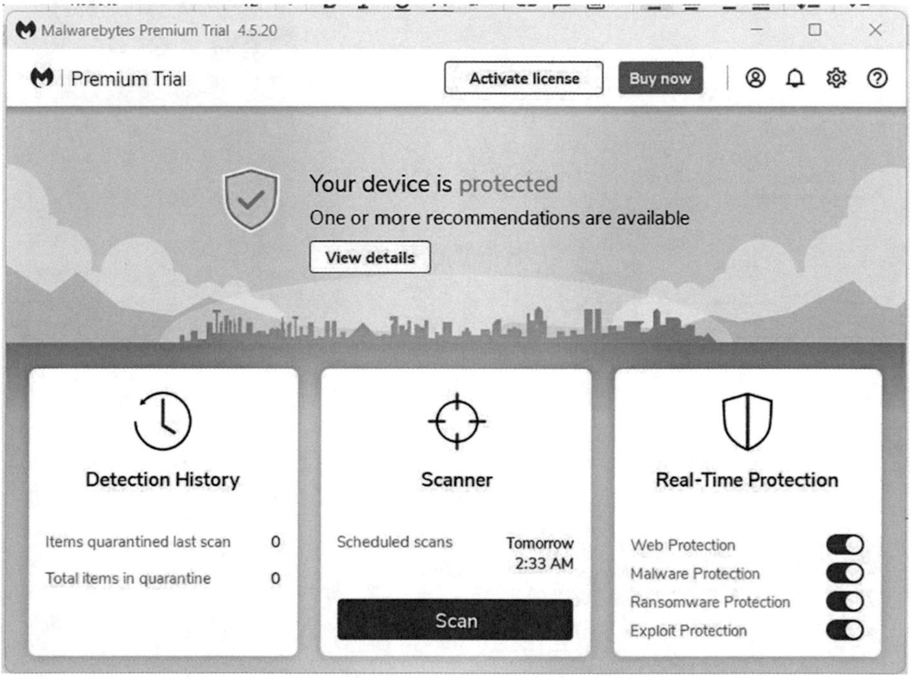


***Figure 8-8.*** *Malwarebytes console*

Figure 8-9 depicts an active scan and Figure 8-10 shows the results from our recent scan. This scan took 3 minutes to complete and had 12 findings. To remove the findings, click the Quarantine button on the bottom right of the screen. By default, Malwarebytes has many of the settings enabled. It automatically checks for, and installs updates every hour. It is set to scan weekly with the ability to adjust this to daily if desired and has real-time scanning enabled. Other anti-malware programs exist and are successful at removing malicious files. Malwarebytes has been tried and true for many years and continues to lead in this space. If you haven't played around with Malwarebytes or another reputable anti-malware software before, it is a good tool to add to your arsenal of detection and eradication applications.

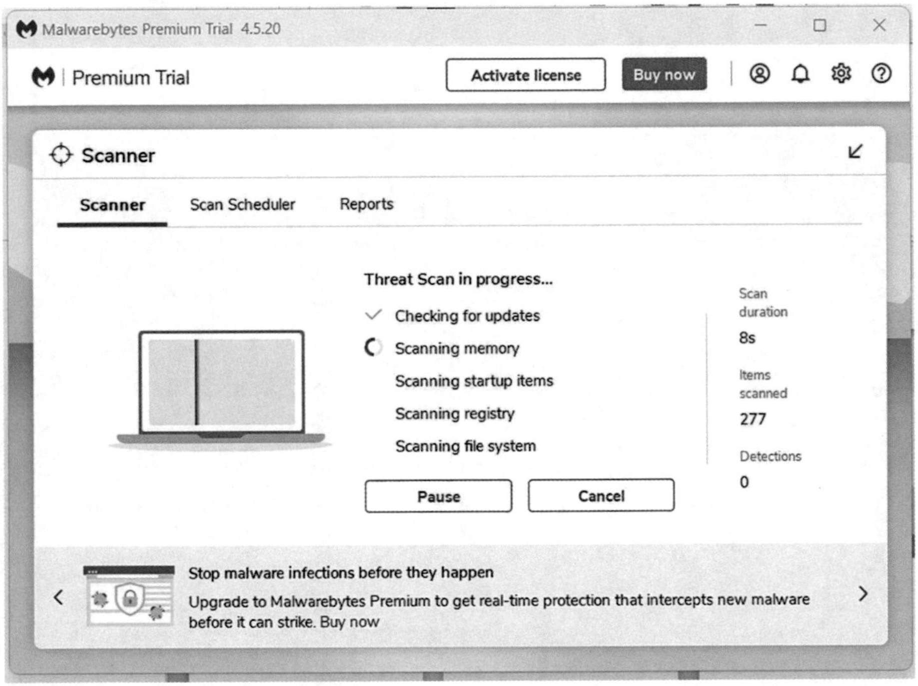


***Figure 8-9.*** *Malwarebytes scan running*

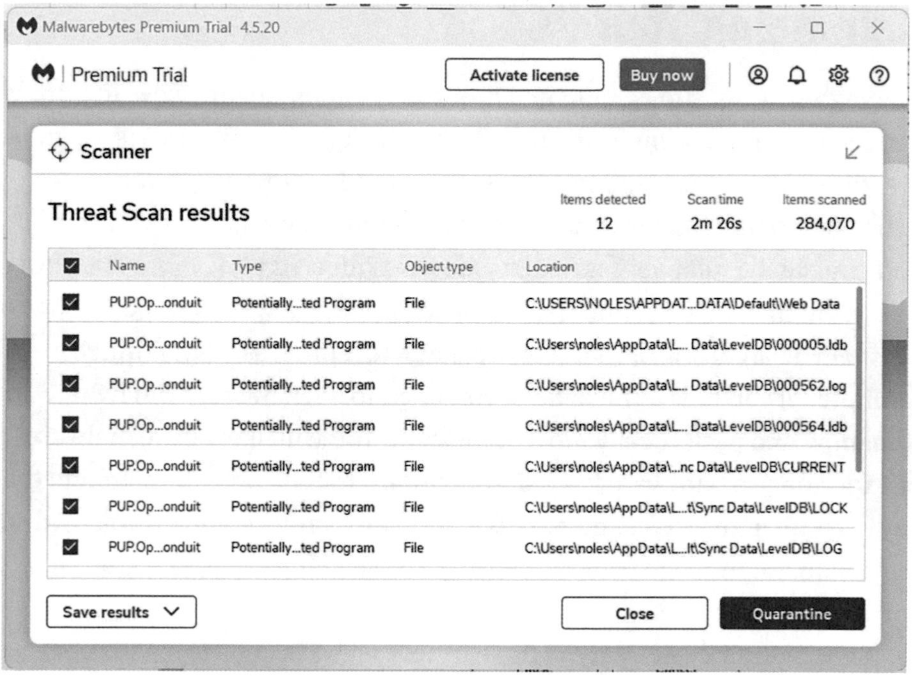


***Figure 8-10.*** *Malwarebytes scan results*

In some cases, malware is so severe and sophisticated that it cannot be removed by antivirus or anti-malware programs. In this case, I recommend the nuclear option, which involves reimaging the computer. This removes all installed files and provides a fresh operating system install. By doing this, you lose any data stored locally on the machine that does not exist on any alternative or cloud-based storage system. It is advised to back up critical data on two different storage platforms and have them physically located in at least two locations. An example would be saving files to a USB or an external hard drive and storing them in a bank vault, at a relative's house, or in a data storage facility.

# Reimaging Your PC

Reimaging or resetting a machine is one of the most secure ways to remove a malicious application from an end-user device. However, this is the most drastic and time-consuming process that could remove important data you failed to back up elsewhere. The operating system gets a fresh start, and you can be relatively sure that whatever infected you before does not infect you moving forward. The Windows operating system is likely what most of you are using, and they have made this process easy. A quick reminder, if you have critical data, you need to back this up somewhere right now and periodically moving forward. You will likely have malware or experience a hardware issue at some point in time on your machine that could result in the loss of data. This should also only be done if you own the pc, do not reimage your employer-provided laptop without checking with the IT department.

Reimaging a device can be done in several ways and varies slightly based on your operating system version. Windows allows you to remove or attempt to keep all your files and transfer them to a fresh install. It is still advised to save critical files regardless of which option you choose.

You can find your operating system by navigating to the My Computer settings or reviewing any documentation you received with the computer. Chances are you are running Windows 7, 10, or 11. Start by searching for the Windows Settings in your Windows search box. Once on the main settings page, you can select the Recovery menu option and be brought to the screen in Figure 8-11.

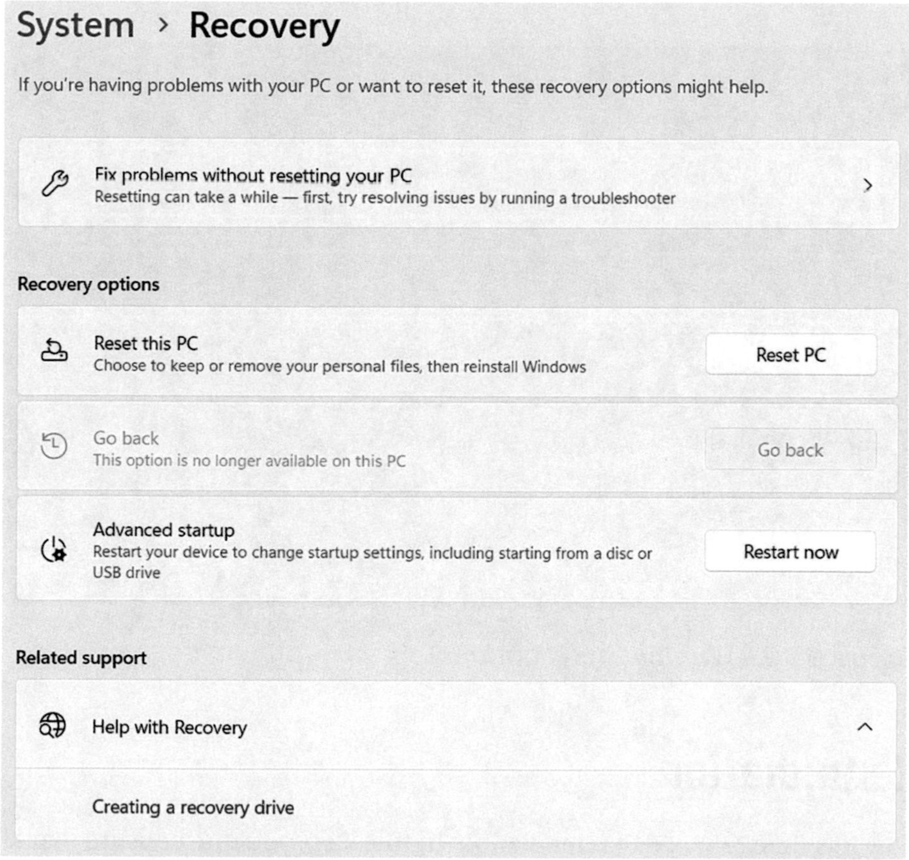


***Figure 8-11.*** *Windows reset PC*

The image in Figure 8-12 shows two options for resetting your device. The first attempt is to save your files and applications. When the device is booted up, it will likely look similar to how you left it. The problem is that if the malicious application isn't removed, it can remain stored on your device and execute again. The malicious file executing could reinfect your machine and bring you back to square one. The remove everything option is preferred, removing all files and applications and providing a fresh start. It is difficult for the malware to remain on the device with a fresh restart. Upon resetting the PC, you should ensure that functionality is resumed, and you can begin restoring necessary applications and files.

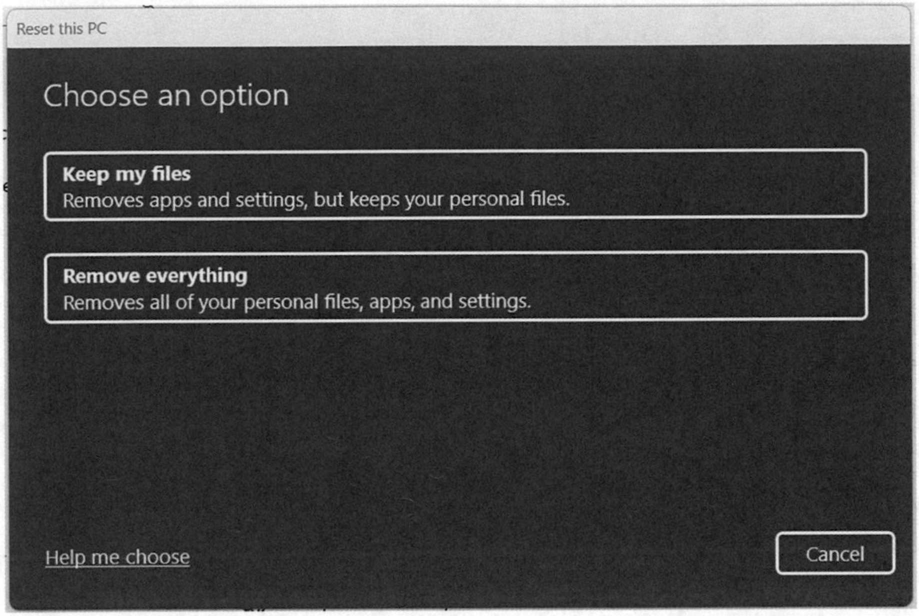


***Figure 8-12.*** *Windows reset options*

# Remediation

Now it is time to move to remediation. In this step, you must ensure that all artifacts are removed from the machine or network and that the impacted device or devices are restored to a good known and operational state. You want the impacted devices to return to the same or better state before the incident, with the same permissions, features, and applications needed to perform the intended purpose. This is a critical component of an organization's incident response plan and is designed to return operations to normal after an incident has occurred.

Eradication focuses on removing the artifacts left by malicious software or actors. Now let's focus on restoring access, fixing any identified vulnerabilities, and hardening the system to prevent this from happening again. Once the malicious software or artifacts are removed, complete the following remediation steps.

1. Install all available software updates. The most critical software updates are Windows operating system updates, called Windows Update. You should then focus on installed application updates.

2. Confirm necessary accesses. Make sure you can visit the necessary sites, local resources, and network resources. You are striving to have the same privileges and accesses you had before. Nothing more and nothing less.

3. Harden the system. This is where you need to install additional security programs or processes as needed.

## Windows Updates

Periodically updates are released containing bug fixes, security updates, and new features for the Windows operating system. These fixes can sometimes address security or configuration issues and vulnerabilities that have been identified and impact Windows operating systems. The updates must be installed and run on the local computer, often requiring a reboot to complete the update process. Microsoft releases updates on a monthly interval, currently on the second Tuesday of every month. It is often called Patch Tuesday, the day when all available patches for the month are released. Microsoft also releases patches that are deemed critical or emergency in nature outside of the Patch Tuesday cycle. This is less common but does happen.

The update process involves downloading and installing updates onto a user's device to keep their system up-to-date and secure. The updates are usually installed automatically, but users can manually check for and install updates. Windows users can quickly check the status of their last update, any missing updates, and the next scheduled update. In the

Windows search box, type **Windows Update**. You are brought to a screen that shows your update status and allows you to check or install updates. Figure 8-13 shows a system that has all available patches installed.

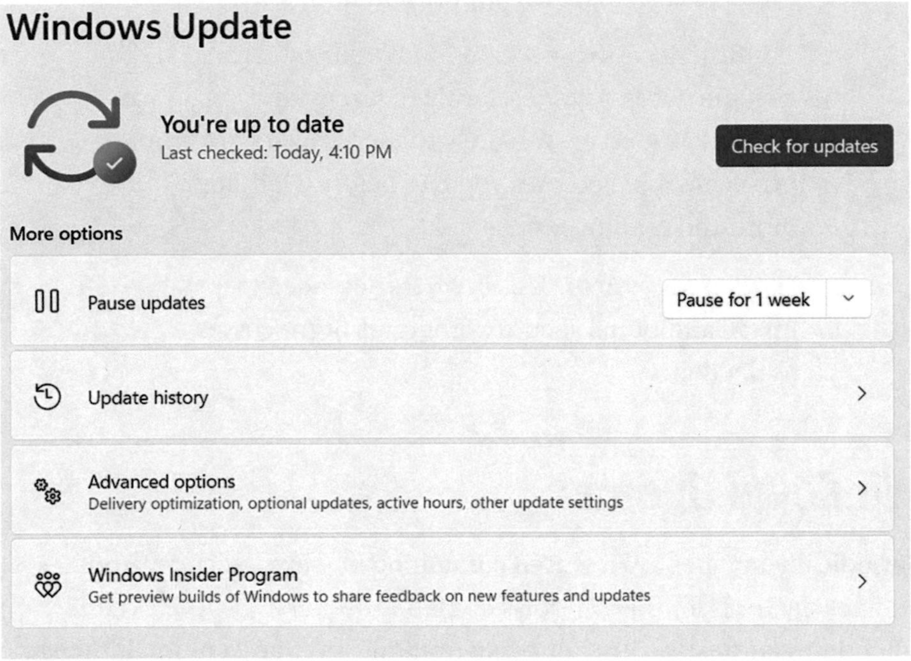


***Figure 8-13.*** *Windows updates applied*

It is impossible to have a system that is updated at all times. The updates need time to be downloaded and applied to the system. Errors with downloads or installation files will occur, so checking for updates periodically or when a major cyber event occurs is a good practice. Figure 8-14 shows a system that is missing two updates. On the right, the top update encountered an error; the one below is pending a restart. You can fix this issue by clicking the Restart now button. It is good practice to check your update status again after the reboot to ensure the patches were correctly installed.

***Figure 8-14.*** *Windows updates missing*

Updating your operating system is critical to preventing and hardening your system. These updates fix known issues and vulnerabilities and must be done regularly. Failure to apply patches correctly results in additional breaches over time.

Once the patches have been applied, testing the system's functionality is important. This is where the user needs to log back into the device and ensure you have all the necessary access needed. Can you browse the web pages you want to access? Can you open the files and folders that you need? Are you able to print? Can you download and install files if needed? These settings must be restored to ensure that the computer is returned to a good known state with the proper accesses in place.

## Lessons Learned

Reflecting on the lessons you learned is the final step in the process, where you take a step back, look at what happened, how you responded, and what you can do to improve our process moving forward. It focuses on past security incidents and identifying areas for improvement to better prepare for and respond to future incidents. This keeps your process continuously improving, making it better and harder for attackers to successfully exploit and steal your data.

To be effective, you should focus on a few key simple elements. These work for all shapes and sizes. Let's focus on the following.

- What went wrong
- What went right
- What you can do to improve the process moving forward

One key aspect of lessons learned is incident analysis, which involves reviewing the details of past incidents to identify the root cause and understand how the incident occurred. It can include analyzing log files, network traffic, and other forensic data to determine the scope of the incident, the systems and data that were affected, and the actions taken to respond to the incident. Where are you missing any information? Would you benefit from more tools? Did you miss some critical data? Incident analysis is important because it helps organizations to understand the nature of the incident and identify areas for improvement in their incident response plans and protocols.

You should evaluate the overall process, including the effectiveness of the incident response process and identifying areas for improvement. This can include evaluating the timeliness and effectiveness of incident detection, the appropriateness of the response, and the effectiveness of incident containment and eradication. Did you stop the incident from spreading? Did you have the right tools to remove the malware and update our system? How can you make this process faster or better? Incident response evaluation is critical because it allows organizations to identify areas for improvement in their incident response plans and protocols and make changes to better prepare for future incidents.

A final aspect of lessons learned is sharing information and best practices with other organizations or people. This can include sharing information about the incident, the actions taken to respond to it, and the lessons learned, as well as sharing best practices for incident response and vulnerability management. Sharing information and best practices is important because it helps other organizations better prepare for and respond to security incidents and can help improve the industry's overall security.

Finally, the lessons-learned process should include the incident's documentation, the actions taken, and the outcome. This help to track the progress and improvements made over time and can be used as a reference for future incident.

In conclusion, lessons learned in cybersecurity are a critical process that allows organizations and people to reflect on past security incidents and identify improvement areas to better prepare for and respond to future incidents. It involves analyzing the details of past incidents, assessing the effectiveness of the incident response, identifying areas for improvement, and sharing information and best practices with other organizations. By implementing effective lessons-learned processes, you can improve incident response capabilities, reduce the likelihood and impact of security incidents, and better protect systems, networks, and data. Additionally, it is important to note that lessons learned are an ongoing process that requires constant monitoring and review to ensure that the organization is always prepared and ready to respond to security incidents.

# Summary

You've come a long way, and it's time to finish strong. Lessons learned in cybersecurity are a critical process that allows organizations and people to reflect on past security incidents and identify improvement areas to better prepare for and respond to future incidents. This involves analyzing the details of past incidents, assessing the effectiveness of the incident response, identifying areas for improvement, and sharing information and best practices with other organizations. By implementing effective lessons-learned processes, you can improve incident response capabilities, reduce the likelihood and impact of security incidents, and better protect systems, networks, and data. Additionally, it is important to note that lessons learned are an ongoing process that requires constant monitoring and review to ensure that you are always prepared and ready to respond to security incidents.

You now have the proper training and information to *catch a phish!* Remember, this is a continuous and evolving process that requires repetition and diligence. Stay vigilant and always be learning. Attackers tend to modify techniques. With the skills you have learned here, you are now ready to begin phishing and help protect others!

# Index

## A



## B



## C



## D



## E, F




N. Oles, *How to Catch a Phish*, https://doi.org/10.1007/978-1-4842-9361-4

## G



## H



## I, J



## K



## L

## Y, Z

Printed in the United States
by Baker & Taylor Publisher Services